Aan: Johan en Sunette
en Kinders

Van: Jacques & Petro

Baie liefde en seën-
wense vir die toekoms
in die Vreemde. X X

Matt 28: 20

Ek is by julle al die
dae tot die voleinding!

G000059505

IT COST ME AN ARM AND A LEG

Braam Louw

Cover image: Tinus Wolmarans, Momento Photography
www.momento.co.za (012) 653-0435

First Edition, 2015
ISBN: 978-1-77605-224-0
e-ISBN: 978-1-77605-223-3

Published by Kwarts Publishers
www.kwarts.co.za

DEDICATION

First and foremost I dedicate this book to my heavenly Father for giving me the wisdom and inspiration for writing this book.

Then to my family for their love, motivation and support in each and every aspect of my life.

I also dedicate this book to my fellow brothers and sisters whom, despite adversity, continue to live a victorious life through faith.

CONTENTS

INTRODUCTION

"Bedazzled by a cloud of thick smoke and thousands of bright electric sparks, I instinctively knew I had to get as far away as possible from the immediate danger. With all my strength, and adrenalin pumping through my veins, I launched myself from the trampoline on which I was standing. I hit the ground beside the catamaran hard. When I turned around I could hear the strange humming sound of high voltage; a sound I had heard before, walking past an electric installation. The sound, at that moment in time, made no sense to me. My eyes desperately searched the vicinity of the boat, hoping to find my brother and friends…"

Braam Louw, born a healthy child, had to accept loss when his right leg and arm were amputated after an accident when he was fifteen years old. He learned to battle and overcome many obstacles throughout his life with his positive attitude and will to survive. To never give in to defeat. Life itself remains a challenge to those living it, constantly aware of the pressure from society's drive towards success.

THE BEGINNING -
EARLY CHILDHOOD YEARS

I, ABRAHAM JACOBUS LOUW, named after my grandfather, a former judge, was born in the summer of 1969 in Kroonstad, Orange Free State, South Africa. I am the second child of Jacques and Petro Louw, and twenty one months younger than my brother Niël.

My early childhood years have become a bit vague over the years, although what remains in my mind is the fact that I was brought up in a home with an aura of love and tranquillity. We lived on the top floor of a lovely old house beneath green oak trees. I still remember the vivid autumn colours of the leaves forming a carpet under the trees in our garden; and the whistling sound of the wind through the branches still lingers in my mind. As a young boy, I learned the value of life and love from two loving and devoted parents. Niël and I have always been good friends and playmates. We had our share of fun and laughter together.

When Niël went to nursery school I remained at home for a further year or so, after which I joined him. I was always a bit of a homebody. It was therefore very traumatic for me when I had to go to nursery school.

Although I made friends very quickly, I was a little shy and a bit of an introvert. My mother was a primary school teacher and would drop us off on her way to work each day.

During our nursery school years we received annual visits from *Father Christmas* before closing for the holidays. I remember being very afraid of the fat, white bearded man in the red suit who arrived in a red fire truck at our school. My brother had trouble convincing me to leave my secure hiding place behind the piano, so that I could collect my present from *Father Christmas* myself. Maybe I was a little afraid of the unknown and cherished comfort and security?

I became intrigued by scuba diving as a little boy. I watched documentaries by Jacques Cousteau and often played imaginary scuba diving games with my friends, using the jungle gym as my submarine. The sandpit was my ocean, just waiting to be explored. I have always had an active imagination. We also played our share of *Cowboys and Crooks* in the backyard, where the good guys went up against the bad guys in imaginary gun fights. Those days of playing were long and uncomplicated compared to the world from an adult's perspective. Perhaps security can be found in the absence of responsibility? We were just boys growing up, doing what boys were supposed to do, and exploring every aspect of being a child. We were happy children, but also naughty at times, as children are.

When I was approximately five years old, we moved to Kempton Park and lived in a nice, sunny family home. We would spend the next three years or so there. In 1976, I went to Impala Primary School where I developed a keen interest in sports early on in my life. On the first day of school, all the new pupils had to compete in an athletics running event. This enabled the coach to make an early cut-off for the school's athletics team for the coming season. I soon found out that I could run like the wind. I easily made the cut-off and became a proud member of the school's athletics team. I found security in competing. Being involved in sports brought about a sense of acceptance, and thus some respect from my peers.

During those years I grew up like a *normal* boy and made friends with a neighbour's boy, a real little rascal, the son of a former Springbok rugby player. The two of us once burned down an open field of grass close to our homes just for the fun of it. Something I obviously never told my parents about! The raging flames had to be extinguished by two fire trucks which someone had called to the scene. Apart from the one or two, or maybe three incidents, I was a good boy - a boy my parents could be proud of, as they often told me. I made weekly walks of about two kilometres to a shop nearby where I bought sweets with my weekly allowance from my dad; I had an incredible sweet tooth. The change I used for buying fire crackers.

Niël and I, along with our friends, would spend hours on the rugby field after school, kicking around the ball. From an early age, I had always been competitive and physically active. I played rugby for the school team and participated in athletics from Grade 1. We used to hold *serious* rugby matches in our garden and played for the *Currie Cup*. This was an empty, silver painted *OROS* bottle. These games were quite competitive and often ended with a few cuts and bruises. A friend of Niël once tackled me during a match and my head slammed against a flowerpot in our garden; my brother left the scene fearing the worst. When I felt the warm blood running down my neck, I ran into the house and told my mother that I had had a *little accident*. She was shocked when she saw the blood gushing from of the open wound and rushed me to the bathroom to try and stop the bleeding. Once the bleeding was more or less under control, she took me to the hospital. During the trip, I remember mumbling, "I do not want stitches", while a friend had to keep a towel pressed to my head to keep the bleeding under control. Despite my protests I ended up with six stitches, due to the laceration on my scalp. The next Saturday, we continued our rugby game.

All in all, my childhood years were not without incidents or *minor accidents*. All normal boys experience them while growing up. For instance, I had my fair share of bicycle accidents; and once broke a front tooth when crossing a trampoline on my bicycle, much to the amusement of the bystanders. I just wanted to find out if it was possible to cross a trampoline on a bicycle with one of my friends jumping on it at the same time. I soon found out however that this was not a good idea. Luckily, I never broke a limb in any of my ordeals, but did often end up with cuts and bruises which healed without any complications. At another time, I had a bicycle accident when my toe got caught in the spikes of the front wheel of my bicycle, and my brother, who was following close behind on his bicycle, could not stop in time and rode over my thigh. It left me with a bloody mouth and bruised leg. I also suffered many small skateboard and roller skating injuries. I mostly administered my own first aid with the help of some *Dettol* to disinfect the wounds, and some plasters and tissues to stop the bleeding. I grew up tough and refused to cry even when in pain. Not that I was ever discouraged from crying by my parents. My father has always been an emotional person himself.

Niël and I never had formal swimming lessons, and during this period in my life, we learned to swim on our own when visiting our neighbour's swimming pool. We soon swam like fish in the water and spent many fun filled afternoons in the swimming pool, diving out coins from the bottom.

When I was about six, my sister Marilie was born. I remember my brother and I praying for a sister every night before we went to bed after we heard that our mother was expecting. Our prayers were answered and my beautiful little baby sister was born.

We were always, to my mind, the perfect family. Early on, my parents told me about God's love for me and His plan for my life as one of His children on earth. A fact which, only later in my life came into full effect. From a very young age, I realised the value of a strong upbringing and gained confidence, which was a result of understanding and supporting parents. They devoted much of their time and energy to our early childhood development. Those were the days when children were brought up solely by their parents, without the assistance of books. My parents have always been, and still are the perfect parents God entrusted to me.

I have always been fond of pets and have had many different kinds; fish, mice, rats, hamsters, bunnies and dogs, at different times in my life. I remember when I was still very young, being chased by a Great Dane while on the way to the shops. He escaped his owner's yard when they accidently left open their front gate. As one can imagine, I didn't really have a fair chance of escaping the galloping beast. Despite my running like never before, he soon caught up with me when I stumbled and fell down. He then nearly licked me to death while standing over me. I was left with a few cuts and scratches mostly as a result of the fall. I was also overwhelmed by the size of the dog and a bit shaky after the experience.

My mother was the musically talented person in our family and enrolled Niël and myself for piano lessons at a young age. She enrolled us to develop our interest in the music world. We each received our own little keyboards, and were initially very keen on this idea. But the daily practice sessions when compared to playing outside soon got the better of us. Needless to say, we never got very far with the piano. We also had a few guitar lessons from my mom who was a talented guitar player and teacher. But like with the piano, we never put any real effort into it.

My brother and I, along with a group of friends once participated in a fun run in which we won medals.

When I was nine years old, we moved to Pretoria and I became a pupil at Skuilkrans Primary School, starting in Grade 4. Once again, I found it difficult adapting to new surroundings and making new friends.

I did not like drastic changes in my life, and tended to cling to the known and familiar. Just like nursery school however, I had no choice in the matter. Dad's work forced him to make this sudden move. Fortunately though, I soon made friends through my participation in sporting events. I became a member of the rugby team and participated in almost all athletics track events.

My brother and I would get up early for practice before school and then stayed after school to continue practicing. From an early age, we were very competitive when participating in sporting events. Because my brother was older and participated in an older age group, we usually ended up playing rugby against each other during practice. The smell of the freshly cut grass of the playing field will forever be imprinted on my senses, just as I will never forget the crispiness of the morning frost under my bare feet during the cold winter mornings. During our lunch breaks, some of the most competitive rugby games unfolded on the rugby field. These games were played with neither rules nor referees. The group of eager participants nominated two captains who then chose their team members from the remaining boys. The stronger and more athletic boys were usually selected first, with the rest being divided between the two teams to ensure fair competition. After the kick-off, the brutal war which left many casualties began. These games were played in our school uniforms and usually ended in torn sleeves and lost shirt buttons; to the agony of many parents. These were the times when boys became men, and where future rugby heroes were born. We were like gladiators, regardless of who won, and proudly left the playing field at the end of each lunch break.

In Grade 6, I developed a keen interest in hurdles. This would forthwith be the event I would spent most of my time on. There was something about the rhythm and the pace, combined with the speed and agility that drew my interest. For me there was always a link between devotion and ultimately reaching success. This link can be drawn between almost all aspects of life. My sister started Grade 1 the same year I became a prefect in Grade 7. She proudly told her friends about her older brother. I suppose she found some comfort in me being there with her.

Like all teenagers, I enjoyed birthday parties and sleeping over at friends. We had pool parties and enjoyed the activities most teenagers did. We loved horror movies, even though it scared us to death when we had to ride our bicycles home afterwards in the dark. Homework and attending class was however not my top priority.

During my primary school years I spent most of my allowance on sweets until I discovered and developed an interest in arcade games, much to the frustration of my parents who felt I was wasting money. I convinced them however that playing arcade games played a major role in the development of my hand to eye co-ordination, which is something I still believe today.

Although not being an avid reader during my younger years, I did read a few *Trompie* books in my spare time. And just like my hero in the books, I got involved in a fist fight or two. In general, I was not an aggressive child. I would rather try to keep the peace and avoid conflict, but I also knew how and when to stand my ground if circumstances demanded. I am not sure whether I ever told my parents about these incidents and believe they were all part of growing up, and growing up is very often tough.

In 1983 I enrolled at Die Wilgers High School. Here my interest and ability in sporting activities only increased. Once again, I was selected for both the athletics and rugby teams. I got rugby boots and athletic *spikes*. My mother spent many of her afternoons driving me around to practice.

At the end of 1983 I qualified for the final hurdles event in the Northern Transvaal's Athletics Championships at Pilditch. I knew the first three athletes would ultimately join the Northern Transvaal's Athletics Team, and I further knew the time required to win this event was well within my reach. I could smell victory.

I found a kind of exhilaration, competing in sporting events, which is difficult to explain in words. Whether it is the cheering of the crowd and the atmosphere in the stadium; or the inner struggle to be the best of the best, or the best you can be, is unclear to me. There is just something magical in being a member of the team, or perhaps just being a member of society, doing what I love and trained for. I can still remember that butterfly in the stomach feeling before an event, and the sense of satisfaction and relief after I completed the race. Maybe the fear of losing, or the fear of disappointing those who placed their trust in me played a roll, I don't know. All I knew was that I wanted to compete, and compete I did!

My grandfather, also a former athlete and keen sports enthusiast, stood with the rest of my family when I lined up for the final hurdles event that year. I was proud, just like always, of having them in the stands. My heart pounded in my chest when I settled into my blocks. I focused on the work at hand and the noise of the crowd disappeared just before I heard the shot. I had an astonishingly quick start and during the first half of the race I saw out of the corner of my eye that I was in a fairly good position to win the event. Unfortunately, I lost my rhythm and stumbled over one of the hurdles. And although I kept on powering my way to the finishing line, I came in fourth overall. My dream of joining the Northern Transvaal's Athletic team, was in ruins. It was obviously a great disappointment for me after spending so many hours on practice and preparation. Where did I go wrong? Fortunately, my parents helped me come to terms and supported and comforted me during this time. They convinced me to try again the following year. My coach also encouraged me to forget the disappointment and move on. I dealt with it; I decided to move on, and practice even harder the next year!

During this stage in my life, I unwillingly learned that there were times when I would fall. Courage, I determined, wasn't defined by how many times I fell, but by how quickly I stood up and regained momentum after falling, with my eyes focused only on the ultimate goal. The lesson I learned through this, was something that would make sense only later in my life, when faced with a lot more than losing an athletics event.

Life, in many aspects, can be compared to an athlete running a race. Niël once said, "It is not the arm which I have lost that really matters, but the countless blessings I have gained in the race of life." Taking these words into account, we will sometimes lose, but will ultimately win or gain something worth much more by going through the experience. This in fact means that losing sometimes ends up being the greatest victory.

This is exactly what the Bible teaches us. We are all running in the race of life. People ran it before us and others will follow. The triumphant participants, who have already finished the race, are the spectators along our way, urging us on to keep on track and to finish successfully, just as they did. During the race, we will encounter a variety of obstacles in many different shapes and sizes, which we will need to overcome. Overcoming these obstacles by the grace and power of God will strengthen us physically and spiritually on our journey, and will ultimately enable us to finish and be victorious.

During the race we need to focus on God in order to stay on track. Losing focus could cause a person to stumble and fall. When running the race, one does not have to be a talented athlete, only a person saved by God's grace, and determined to finish the race as Jesus did...

I started practicing again early in 1984, even though there were no Northern Transvaal Colours available for my age group, and at the end of the year qualified for the Northern Transvaal's Athletics Championships again. This only meant that I would participate in an older age group and I decided to leave my decision to the coming year...

CHRISTMAS TIME - VACATION TIME

URING MY CHILDHOOD years, I was privileged enough to spend almost every December holiday at my grandfather's beach cottage *Uhuru* in Buffalo Bay, in the Southern Cape. This is where I learned to appreciate a small part of the beauty that is God's creation. That beauty emphasized by the cool coastal breeze and the endless rolling and rumbling of the incoming waves from the Indian Ocean. I will always treasure the scent of *Sour fig* flowers and the unmistakable smell of suntan lotion on a hot summer's day under the African sky. The tingling of the cold sea spray on my skin when entering the waves for the first time on a breezy summer morning will always remain close to my heart.

This is where I realized what it means to live life to the fullest, to be thankful and to appreciate every day. Ultimately, to live every day of my life as if it were my last.

I remember spending hours on the beach, sitting and running around. Climbing up and down sand dunes and thinking of my life, appreciating what I had and thankful for the many blessings I had received up until then. I was blessed in so many ways, and really experienced God's love and purpose for my life in a variety of ways.

In short, life was good...

As a teenager, I had the opportunity to spend long summer holidays with my family and made many friends on the coast. I soon became one of the locals down there. Ultimately, I used the time to evaluate the purpose of my life, and the reason for my existence. I spent time preparing myself physically and mentally for the coming year. And of course, I used the time just to relax and be lazy on the beach, under the African sky and have the occasional ice cream, or hamburger and chips take-away.

In 1984, Niël and I received our Christmas presents a month earlier than usual - a brand new paddle ski for each of us. Our parents gave them to us earlier so that we could practice before going on holiday to the beach. Riding the wave ski's required a lot of rhythm and balance, so we honed our skills in the swimming pool at home until we were near perfect.

We were now ready to take on the mighty waves of the Indian Ocean!

Christmas each year was a time to spend with other family members, and although many shared the beach cottage, there were just as many actually residing as close as Brenton and George. On Christmas Eve, we sang carols around a beautifully decorated Christmas tree, which we picked from the Knysna forest and exchanged gifts. We had a wonderful time sharing in the feast around a huge dining room table, lit by candles and paraffin lamps. Christmas Eve was wonderful, although as a child I could not wait to open the Christmas presents. I learned from a very young age that the presents were mainly there to remind us of what Jesus has done for us.

The children usually went out on Christmas Eve to climb the highest dune on the main beach, to kill some time before we started opening the Christmas presents. My mother usually led the singing with her guitar and the rest of us followed, each in his or her own peculiar voice. The silence of the night was filled with the sound of familiar Christmas Carols. Even the neighbours' singing could be heard over the ever pounding distant sound of the raging waves against the rocks on the nearby beach.

Before we opened Christmas presents, my grandfather a former pastor, read the Christmas story from his Bible while everyone sat around the dining room table. The flames from the paraffin lamp formed dancing shadows on the room's inner walls.

This was Christmas time, as I have known it for many years. It was also a time to think about the less fortunate.

Once home after attending the Christmas day service at the local wooden church, we quickly changed into our bathing suits and headed down to the beach to indulge in the soothing summer sun.

Not only have I been blessed with a talent for sporting events, such as athletics and rugby - I was also drawn to water sports like surfing, body boarding, water skiing and wave skiing. Since I can remember, I've followed surfing competitions on the television and actual surfers on the waves with the utmost interest and admiration for their technique and skills. In a way, their way of life always reminded me of the way we are supposed to live, taking on huge waves that come our way with guts and making the most of every opportunity. It therefore seems as if there is indeed an important link between surfing and living our lives as Christians.

Being so interested in water sports, I received a body board during my early teens as a gift. I would spend hours on the waves with the locals, hundreds of meters from the beach, on the well known sand bank, where the water was shallow and the natural reef created the best surf break. Although living inland, I quickly became a well known face amongst the local surfers, trying out new tricks on the waves every summer vacation as the years went by. I once met a lovely surfer girl on the beach named Tania, with whom I spent most of my summer vacation, chatting about this and that and riding waves together. The bigger the waves, the greater the challenge. Out there on the surf I could really live out my dreams and conquer my greatest fears.

Surf's up!

My interest in body boarding later developed into an interest for paddle skiing. Sitting on the ski, I could more easily see the approaching waves and manoeuvre myself into the face of the rolling wave with the oars to catch the biggest one out there! I soon realized that I had quite a talent for this sport. Words and phrases like "off the lip" and "riding the tube" soon became part of my everyday "vacation language". I became a fan of surfing brand names like "Rip Curl", "Billabong" and "Lizzard", if only I could get the sponsorship to go with it. Maybe one day, I thought? A movie named "Pointbreak" became one of my favourites.

I can still remember the burning sensation of the hot sand under my feet when I left my flip-flops under the umbrella to quickly go and buy an ice cream and the scent of coconut infused tanning oil on bronzed bodies around me. I can still hear the busy, but relaxing sounds of voices and children's laughter when laying back on the beach with closed eyes.

The beach has always been a place that draws families together. It is a place where, whoever you are in "real life" throughout the year becomes irrelevant; where managers of huge firms and "important people" strip down to the bare necessities, in the form of board shorts and bikini's. The athletic ones and the couch potatoes all come together in harmony; everyone out there with only one purpose in mind, to relax…

What more can a teenager wish for? Surf, sun, endless white beaches, and a family to support me in whatever I wished to do to expand my experiences on this planet called Earth…

HOLIDAY PLANNING - 1984

UNLIKE PREVIOUS YEARS, December of 1984 brought a change in the normal routine of getting the family into Dad's car and driving down to the coast for our annual family vacation. My dad only got leave close to Christmas and the arrangement was that he would take down our paddle skis with the remainder of our family. My brother and I would leave earlier.

This year, Niël and I would catch a train to our family in Bloemfontein, and then drive the remainder of the route down with them to Buffalo Bay. Although a bit different from the previous years, the idea of the train trip brought unexpected excitement.

Eager to get down to the coast, we got onto the train at the station, waved goodbye to the family and left for Bloemfontein. After a long but exiting journey, we arrived at Bloemfontein station where we were met by our aunt and uncle. We stayed overnight with them and left early the following morning, heading for Buffalo Bay.

This trip was long and tiresome, but definitely worthwhile, driving through the Karoo and Graaff-Reinet with its wonderful historical background and beautiful old church. After refuelling at Graaff-Reinet and a quick lunch at a local coffee shop we were on our way.

Like every other year before, reaching George and knowing that Buffalo Bay was just around the corner, made the long journey and stiff joints well worth the drive. The air felt moist and sticky, and we could already smell the crisp salty air of the Indian Ocean. The last few kilometres down the coast with its beautiful dense vegetation, although a pretty sight, felt awfully long that year.

Reaching the beach cottage that year brought the same sense of wellbeing I had experienced so many times before. We arrived early on the morning of 8 December 1984, and had the whole day to explore the beaches and relax after the long journey. I must admit, I had slept part of the journey and suddenly felt very energetic in the familiar coastal surroundings.

My brother and I shared the bottom room of the cottage. Opening the door to our room for the first time that year, brought the well-known and comforting smell of musky timber wood, drenched in moist coastal air, mixed with the unmistakable sweet smell of mothballs and insect repellent. The narrow, dark humid corridor leading to our bathroom, although a bit scary, also brought many comforting memories. I could see the flames of the gas geyser dancing inside the appliance after I lit it. The windows of our room were murky because of the humid and salty coastal air. "We have arrived!", I thought. Eagerly, we unpacked our suitcases, reached for our *baggies* and beach towels, and headed down barefoot on the familiar narrow cobble road leading to the main beach. Like a flash it was summer and time for vacation again. Soon I would be 15 years old. I threw down my towel on the beach and felt the warm sand burning the soles of my feet as I ran towards the invitingly cold sea water. When I reached the first whitewash of the waves breaking close to shore, all the worries about the past exams were washed from my mind. I knew I had studied hard and had done my best! My brother and I spent an hour or two between the waves catching them to bodysurf.

"Live is a journey, enjoy the ride!" And what a ride it turned out to be!

With board shorts soaked with seawater, and beach sand clinging to wet feet and ankles, we walked back to the cottage only to be met on our way by our school friends, Hennie and Cronnie Beukes. We knew that they had also planned a family vacation at the well known, and popular caravan park in Buffalo Bay, although we thought that they would only arrive a week or two later. Quickly, and with excitement in the air we exchanged our initial plans for the holiday. We decided to meet up again later that evening after supper to socialize and discuss further plans.

After supper we anxiously headed down to the caravan park situated next to the beach, about a twenty minute walk from the cottage. On arrival we were warmly welcomed by our friend's parents, Gert and Ansie Beukes. We were invited to participate in a card game with them and enjoyed a cup of hot, steamy coffee with a view of the surf. We spent a wonderful evening in the company of close friends. Later that evening we discussed the possibility of going sailing on their catamaran later during the holiday. We first had to get our parents' approval, but I didn't think it would be a problem. We planned to go sailing as soon as the weather permitted it, taking into account that we needed a fairly strong wind. Hennie and Cronnie were both well acquainted and experienced with the rigging and sailing of their catamaran, and had been for quite some time.

We would only later on finalize the plans, and Hennie would let us know well in advance should the weather be favourable for sailing. When we left their caravan and headed to the cottage, I could feel the anticipation building up inside me. Sailing on the catamaran would be a wonderfully new experience. Previously, I had the opportunity to participate in social sailing with my uncle's small sailboat on the Touws River in the Wilderness. The catamaran however, would be a totally new experience, sailing at high speed on one of the famous lakes in the area. Obviously I was game for this...

A few days before Christmas our parents and sister arrived. We helped them unpack and sat down for supper around the table. In my heart I thanked God for keeping them safe on their long journey, taking into account the high accident rate on the roads. After my father said grace, we sat down and ate in silence, each one busy with their own thoughts, but thankful to be together as a family again, sharing the experience of a summer vacation in our beloved Buffalo Bay. I could see the exhaustion on my father's face, the long journey having taken its toll. From where I was sitting, I could also see the warm orange glow of the setting sun over the shiny bright ocean, slowly disappearing over the horizon, giving rise to the thousands of stars so unbelievably visible down at the coast.

It was only later that evening that I told my parents of our plans to go sailing with our friends. Knowing my parents, I knew that I had to break the news as early as possible, so as to give them ample time to chew on the thought and calculate the risks involved, not that my parents have ever been overprotective. I just knew it would be wise to involve them in our plans early on. Amazingly, they were quite taken with the idea, knowing that our friends were experienced sailors, and that both their sons were strong swimmers.

During the next few days, the idea of sailing scarcely crossed my mind. The weather was sunny and windless and exceptionally good. I worked on my paddle skiing skills now that our brand new paddle skis had arrived with my dad. They had never before tasted salt water. I spent countless hours riding waves at the sand bank close to the caravan park. Hennie, also an experienced paddle skier joined me and my brother on several occasions, helping to improve our skills. Riding the waves at speed with salt water spraying in my eyes and the wind in my hair, made me realize how easy it would be to get addicted to the sport. It was me, fighting against the forces of nature, and eventually being able to execute a 360⁰ degree turn on the face of a wave that made the experience that much more rewarding. Out there I could only rely on the strength of my own arms on the oars against the continuous surge of foaming sea water around me; threatening to overpower me, and drag me over the sharp rock reef so close to the breaking waves.

Although a bit of an adrenalin junkie, I always calculated the risks involved in any activity I undertook. Riding waves was only one of the experiences I came to love and pursue. The future looked bright for me in so many sporting activities. There and then, I decided to start early the following year with athletics practice. I wanted to be the best I could be.

Or perhaps even the best of the best.

On 24 December 1984, we had the privilege of celebrating my mother's birthday at the coast. She had been born on the day before Christmas and always playfully complained that the family wouldn't be able to afford a present for her, seeing as 24 December was Christmas Eve, the time to exchange Christmas presents. As with previous years there was no reason for her concern. On the morning of her birthday we used to go into our parents' bedroom, this year being no exception, and sat down on their bed, while my mother opened her presents. These moments were always filled with tears of joy and laughter.

That afternoon we took a saw and everyone went along to pick a Christmas tree, as we have done in previous years, from the Knysna forest. We quickly started decorating the tree when we got home with all the handmade decorations and arranged the presents under the tree. My sister had the privilege of taping down the angel on the top of the tree that year. That evening we sat down around the tree and every child got a turn to read a verse from the Scriptures about the well known, lovely story of the Child being born in Bethlehem.

The following morning I woke up with the Christmas carols of the previous evening still lingering in my mind. "How quickly time goes by", I thought. I glanced at my wristwatch and got dressed for the Christmas sermon at our local church. One of my father's favourite Christmas songs came to mind: "I'm dreaming of a white Christmas …"

The rest of the day went by without any major differences when compared to previous years. After the sermon we went to the beach to soak up the rays and work on our suntan.

That evening we received a visit from Hennie and Cronnie, telling us the weather forecasted for the next day would be perfect for sailing. With all the formalities of Christmas behind us, the timing felt just right! According to the weather broadcasts on the radio channels, the sky would be overcast with fairly strong south-western winds blowing along the coastal region…

After telling our parents about our plans, all was set for the following day's activities. My dad would wake us up early, so that we could have breakfast before we left. Cronnie, Hennie, and their father would meet us at the cottage with the catamaran on its trailer. From there we would travel together to our destination, preferably Rondevlei or Swartvlei, two of the most well-known lakes in the area.

SWARTVLEI - 1984

ON THE MORNING of 26 December, my brother and I got up when we heard our father's voice outside our door calling us for breakfast, which was normally served at the dining room table. Anticipating the day ahead, I didn't really have much of an appetite, and gulped down my coffee knowing that our friends would soon arrive. When we heard their car approaching we grabbed our towels and went outside to meet them. We were all dressed in T-shirts and board shorts. Despite the overcast weather, the temperature outside was still fairly warm and humid and I could feel a soft breeze blowing from the sea when I left the cottage.

We unanimously decided that Swartvlei would be the best place to go sailing, taking into account the vast openness of the well known tourist site. Swartvlei was about 45 kilometres from Buffalo Bay, and would take us approximately twenty five minutes to reach with the catamaran on the trailer.

On our way there, we would pass Goukamma and Groenvlei. We would then take a sharp right turn towards Swartvlei at Bleshoender Station just after Sedgefield, driving on a narrow gravel road before crossing the railway line. That specific spot was quite popular amongst sailing enthusiasts and we had passed that spot many times.

During the journey we were all very quiet. I'd been on those roads many times before with my parents and every kilometre that passed brought back certain memories. We had visited Sedgefield many times in the past, and I knew that I'd seen the sign for *Bleshoender Station* next to the road on the way to George before. The narrow road from Buffalo Bay lead to the N2 highway. The N2 followed the coastline all the way from the North Coast of Natal, through Transkei, East London, and Port Elizabeth along the Garden Route to Knysna and eventually to Cape Town. Swartvlei was situated next to the N2 between Sedgefield and Wilderness.

At that time of the year the fields along the road were green and appeared soft and fluffy as we drove past. Those areas are well known for their pine plantations, and home to the Knysna elephant. Driving past Groenvlei, I saw the sails of some wind surfers and yachts that looked like butterflies on a pond. Reaching the N2, I knew we were now close to our destination. We only had a few kilometres left before we would reach our destination. Although very excited and full of energy, the trip itself calmed me down.

Upon reaching our destination, we found that we weren't the only people taking advantage of the lovely windy day for sailing. The last fifty meters of the gravel road leading to the water was crowded with all the yachts, catamarans and vehicles that were parked everywhere.

We crossed the railway lines and parked our vehicle some distance from the other holiday goers, got out and unhooked the trailer. Our friend's dad gave us a hand with rigging the sails, attaching it to the boom, securing the mesh trampoline and adjusting the rudder. The mast was erected and the stability cables connected; two cables leading down to the front beam.

After everything was set up, our friend's dad got into his car and drove away… I can still remember him waving through the window as he crossed the railway lines on his way out. He would come back for us later that afternoon.

Before we put on our life jackets, my brother took out his camera to capture the moment, and the rest of us posed on the catamaran. Sitting on the catamaran, I suddenly got that same butterfly feeling in my stomach I had experienced many times before running a race. Would this experience be the same?

Everything was set and we were ready to go!

I was told to stay on the trampoline to balance the boat while the sails started bulging with the wind. Cronnie pushed from behind and Niël and Hennie dragged from the front beam, each with one hand on the beam, and the other holding on to the front part of the trailer, keeping the wheel from digging into the soft soil.

We slowly began our journey towards the water…

THE UNFORESEEN HAPPENED

BEDAZZLED BY A cloud of thick smoke and thousands of bright electric sparks, I instinctively knew I had to get as far away as possible from the immediate danger. With all my strength and adrenalin pumping through my veins, I launched myself from the trampoline on which I was standing. I hit the ground beside the catamaran hard. When I turned around I could hear the strange humming sound of high voltage; a sound I had heard before, walking past an electric installation. The sound, at that moment in time, made no sense to me. My eyes desperately searched the vicinity of the boat, hoping to find my brother and friends…

With shocked horror I saw my brother lying close to the front beam of the catamaran! His body was arching up and down as a result of an electric current. I could smell burning material and the distinctive odour of sulphur filled the air around me. Instinctively and without a moment's hesitation, I ran towards my brother's body with only one thought in my mind. I had to get him away from the catamaran as soon as possible! I reached out to him with my right hand. Suddenly and unexpectedly, I experienced a feeling, like what I think of as being struck by lightning must feel. I heard a ringing sound and lost consciousness as the world around me went dark…

Seconds went by like hours...

"Hello, hello, can you hear me...?" The words reached my ears as if in a dream. Slowly I opened my eyes and the blurry faces of strangers kneeling beside me slowly took on human form. "Are you ok? Where are you from? Any pain?" All those questions at once! "How did they expect me to answer them?". My lips struggled to form words, they felt swollen and numb just like my tongue. "Had I lost my speech?" I wondered. "Am I in heaven?" I did however feel pain. I could feel the life jacket digging into the soft, tender skin of my right shoulder. I could hear voices coming from nearby. "Where's my brother?" I heard myself asking in a strange voice, as if someone else was asking the question. "He's ok!" Someone replied.

I was still alive, and from where I was lying I could see the hull of the catamaran close by. It was unbelievably quiet, despite the voices of the bystanders. I could no longer hear the humming sound. I also knew that although alive, I was in bad shape. I could see my right arm protruding from my shoulder in a stiff, unfamiliar manner. I was unable to flex my elbow or bend my fingers and the outer layer of skin on my arm looked tender and scorched. I couldn't feel my legs and silently wondered if I was paralyzed. I knew I wouldn't be able to stand up, and had to endure the position in which I was. Looking away from the scene, I could see cars in the distance; parked next to the highway with people getting out in the hope of catching a glimpse of what had happened.

Someone said my arm was broken. "I had never before broken an arm or a leg", I thought. "Is this how it feels?" I only remembered my finger that I broke during a rugby match.

Slowly I turned my head to one side. I could see my brother's legs close by. The next moment though, he jumped up and started running. Someone had to calm him down again. He mumbled unintelligibly. "Are you OK Niël?" I shouted. "I am, and you?" came his reply unexpectedly. I knew then we would make it. We had made it thus far.

Desperately my eyes searched for those of my elder brother. When our eyes locked, just for a few seconds, I felt a little comfort in the midst of the unfamiliar situation.

I could hear Hennie's voice in the distance. I knew that he was OK for the time being.

People were everywhere around us, some praying, others trying to calm us down, and more still with shock on their faces. One woman carefully placed a folded beach towel under my head.

"Where is the ambulance?", I asked a bystander next to me. He, obviously also in shock, told me that the ambulances were on their way. Someone had phoned the hospital. He told me to relax and stay calm. What else could I do?

After minutes which felt like hours, I heard the wailing sirens of approaching ambulances. The sound was comforting under the circumstances, help was on the way.

When the two ambulances arrived everything happened quickly. One of the paramedics approached me with a breathing mask. It was not until then that I realized I was having difficulty breathing. The sweet smell of oxygen filled my nostrils as I sucked down the compressed air which had an almost narcotic effect on me. With the utmost skill and care I was lifted onto a stretcher and taken to the back of the ambulance. They brought Hennie to the same ambulance. This was the first time I had seen him since we had begun to pull the yacht towards the water. Minutes felt like hours. I felt relieved leaving the accident scene behind. What really happened on that beautiful summer morning will forever be a vague memory...

Niël was taken to the other ambulance and we were rushed to hospital. On our way there I could hear the sirens and I could feel the driver speeding. A throbbing pain, previously a dull ache, slowly started creeping up on me. There was a paramedic with us in the back of the ambulance but he only sat there without saying a word or showing any emotion. "He was probably used to this", I thought. Maybe he was taught to react like this, to show no emotion. The silence in the back of the ambulance was suddenly broken when Hennie and I started praying out loud to God to help us to endure the pain. After that I could feel the pain slowly subsiding. I knew then that we were obviously not in control of the situation, but that God was. Drifting away I remembered the well known words of **"Footprints in the Sand"** written by Mary Stevenson:

**"One night a man had a dream. He dreamed
He was walking along the beach with the LORD.
Across the sky flashed scenes from his life.
For each scene he noticed two sets of
footprints in the sand: one belonging
to him, and the other to the LORD.
When the last scene of his life flashed before him,
he looked back at the footprints in the sand.
He noticed that many times along the path of
his life there was only one set of footprints.
He also noticed that it happened at the very
lowest and saddest times in his life.
This really bothered him and he
questioned the LORD about it:
"LORD, you said that once I decided to follow
you, you'd walk with me all the way.
But I have noticed that during the most
troublesome times in my life,
there is only one set of footprints.
I don't understand why when
I needed you most you would leave me."**

The LORD REPLIED:
"My son, my precious child,
I love you and I would never leave you.
During your times of trial and suffering,
when you see only one set of footprints,
it was then that I carried you."

AFTERMATH - FLYING HOME

CRONNIE BEUKES, THE younger of the Beukes brothers, who we later found out sustained no injuries, was taken back to Buffalo Bay where he had the unpleasant task of breaking the terrible news to the two families.

According to my parents, he was very pale when he gave a short hasty description of what happened. My cousin was sent to fetch Marilie, (then nine years old), who was still down on the beach. He told her that her brothers had been in an accident and struggled to answer all the questions she had.

I could feel arms lifting my stretcher out of the ambulance and onto a gurney. Everyone at the hospital did what they had been taught with the utmost precision and avoided making eye contact with me. As I was pushed down a long corridor, I saw the lights on the ceiling speeding by. Everyone was in a hurry and this only made the situation more uncomfortable. I wondered if I could still die? I had no idea at which hospital I was or what would happen next. I could hear hospital nurses and doctors exchanging medical terms but I couldn't understand what they were talking about. In a way, I felt more like a subject than a person. With well-trained hands, my clothes were removed and they put me on a drip. I didn't even feel the prick of the needle; my mind was elsewhere, soaring above. I was pushed into a room where Hennie and my brother were lying. They were asleep as far as I could see. "Where were my parents?", the thought went through my mind. "Will they be angry about what had happened?" "Do they know yet?" I felt confused and disorientated. "Did someone phone my parents?" "Should I try to phone them?" During that confusing time a doctor came into the little room and, as if he could read my mind, told me that my parents were on their way. Before I could ask any of the questions that were laying heavily on my mind, he left the little room.

More time went by...

"Hello Braam!" I heard the well known and familiar voice of my mother calling my name. The same tone of voice I had heard so many times before when I was ill or in distress. I opened my eyes slowly, my eyelids feeling heavy. They were both there dressed in white, like angels from the children's Bible. My dad had his arm around my mother comforting her. I knew looking at me could not be easy for them, or any parent in their situation. There I lay, bandages everywhere and under white sheets. My right arm and leg felt stiff. I wanted to move towards them, touch them, hug them, but could not. My mother, trying to stay strong, kissed me on my cheek. I could see tears building up in her eyes. I was already crying inside. I wanted to say something to comfort her, but I didn't know where to start, or what to say. I could see my dad too, biting his lower lip. He also said a few words. It was a very emotional moment indeed, and probably only a few words were necessary. I heard myself saying: "Don't worry, we will be OK." My mother could no longer hold back the tears. She wiped away a tear rolling down her cheek. "How long are we going to be in hospital?" I asked. There was no reply...

They later informed me that we would be flown back to Pretoria by a Red Cross plane and that everything had been arranged. My parents and Marilie would drive back to Pretoria with my cousin. My uncle, also a doctor, would be waiting for us at the hospital in Pretoria. "Why are we going back?" I thought. "The holiday's not over, is it?" Everything was so confusing... "What about the sailing?" I drifted into a deep sleep.

Later that afternoon emergency procedures were carried out in George Hospital. When I opened my eyes again I was in the back of an ambulance. It was dark and rainy outside, and I could see the body of a plane when looking out the back door of the ambulance. I recognized the silhouettes of my parents as well as my friend's parents walking on the runway in silence. I heard a voice saying "There he comes", and assumed we were waiting for the pilot. My parents came to greet us when we were moved into the plane. They told me that they would meet us in Pretoria, and my mom touched my cheek tenderly. And although my arm seemed swollen, and I could see that it was wrapped in thick white bandages, I had no pain. I then realized a few hours had gone by since the time I had first been with my parents in the small room. A few hours I could not remember and it made me uneasy. I remembered someone saying I would go for an operation before being flown to Pretoria. "What did they do during the operation?" My arm was still intact, although swollen. Maybe it *was* broken.

The door of the plane was shut and I could feel it moving on the runway. Just after take-off, I once again drifted into a deep sleep...

When I opened my eyes again, my arm and leg were in the most excruciating pain I had ever experienced. There was a paramedic next to my bed and I slowly turned my head trying to see if I could get his attention. He looked over when he saw me moving. "I need something for pain". He told me that he had no pain medication with him, and that he had received strict instructions not to give us any. The medication could endanger our internal organs, especially the kidneys. He told me this in a tone very much reminiscent of one of my school teachers giving a lecture. "What could I do?" I had to accept what I was told. After what felt like hours but was probably only another fifty minutes, I could feel the plane descending. I could hear the wheels coming out and then the air brakes when we hit the runway. We landed at Grand Central Airport and were taken by ambulance to the HF Verwoerd Hospital (now Steve Biko Hospital).

On the way to the hospital I fell asleep once more, probably a lingering aftereffect of the anaesthesia from my earlier surgery.

When I opened my eyes I heard voices around me. I could see the familiar and friendly face of my uncle Johan, a medical doctor, standing next to my bed. In a calm voice he informed me that I'd been in a serious accident and had sustained severe internal third degree burns as a result of the electrical shock. He told me that I was in the hands of the best specialists available, in the field of electric burn wounds. One of the specialists had just arrived from overseas. He also informed me that losing part of an arm or leg was a possibility if they were to save my life. His talk of losing limbs made no sense to me at that time and I was shocked. On the other hand, I never realized that my life was still in danger. They were the specialists though and whatever they decided would be the right decision. After he spoke to me, a nurse came into the poorly lit room and began removing the bandages around my right arm. While she was doing this, I realized that I had no sensation left in that arm, and couldn't feel any pain...

With the bandages removed, I stared in horror at what was left of my right arm. Deep incisions had been made across the length of my forearm. I could actually see the muscle and bone inside. Now I knew what had happened to me during the surgery in George. Only the skin on my right hand was untouched. My hand felt distant from me, as if I was looking at someone else's hand. I could not move a finger. The nurse picked up a needle and without hesitation, pushed the needle into the tip of my index finger. Strangely I felt nothing, even with the needle inserted almost a centimetre into the flesh of my finger. I realized the severity of my injuries, and in a way silently accepted that I might lose my hand or arm. The nurse gave me an injection and I fell asleep…

I drifted in and out of consciousness. I had no idea which day it was or what time. Time made no sense to me. I felt like part of the cosmos, drifting around in the universe. Opening my eyes now and then, I could see nurses dressed in white around my bed. Everything was white. It was quiet all the time and the nurses spoke in hushed tones. I could see Niël's body on the bed next to mine, but couldn't speak to him. As soon as it felt like I was regaining consciousness, I received another injection from the nurse, putting me back into *Morphine Wonderland*. This went on for days but felt like weeks. I wasn't aware of my body. Later on, the intervals between the injections became longer. During those times that I regained consciousness, I could feel pain. And still later on, close family members were allowed to visit us. Although I knew they were there, I was unable to speak to them, feeling drowsy all the time.

We received a visit from the surgeon and he informed us that we'd been on morphine injections for the past few days but that these would now be stopped. He told us that the surgery went well, and that he was satisfied with our progress. We were still in the intensive care unit. My only thought though was "What surgery…?"

Now fully conscious, I thought of lifting the blankets to see my body. Although I could feel all my limbs, something felt strange and unfamiliar. I unwillingly, but with a sense of urgency, moved the fingers of my left hand over my chest towards my right shoulder. I could not feel my right arm. I could only feel bandages wrapped around my chest where my arm used to be. My right leg, also wrapped in bandages, ended below the knee in an awkward looking stump. Looking over at Niël I saw that he had lost his left arm and that his left shoulder was also bandaged. I was shocked.

But through the shock there was a strange sense of calm in my findings. Despite everything, I was still alive…

IN RETROSPECT

THE QUESTION REMAINS: "What exactly happened on that summer's day in December of 1984?"

After the traumatic experience, the pieces of the puzzle slowly started falling in place. Some information we obtained came from bystanders who had been present on the day, but that we only met later in life.

When we started pushing the catamaran towards the water, the tip of the aluminium mast, an excellent conductor of electricity, touched an overhead high-voltage power line running alongside the railway tracks. The power line supplied Sedgefield and other neighbouring coastal towns with electricity. An electric current of 11 000 volts surged down the mast and stabilizing cables to the front beam. My brother and Hennie were electrocuted instantly. The current used their bodies as conductors into the ground. When I reached out to grab my brother to get him away from the catamaran, the current went through my body before the power tripped at Sedgefield, which was without electricity for a few hours.

We later found out that employees from the nearby sub-station had seen that the power had tripped, and thought of switching it on again.

Luckily they decided against it in favour of first finding out why the power had tripped.

During those times, many newspaper articles were published with headings like: "City trio operated on after Cape yacht drama", "Boys loses arms, leg, after power shock", "Grim blow for 3 brave boys", "Teen hero saves two from frying" and "Limbless boys making progress". The events leading to the accident, and the progress made thereafter were followed anxiously by the public.

As to our injuries sustained and the consequences thereof, I had to do my own research.

Reading through medical journals, I gained the following valuable information:

Most of the articles confirmed that the severity of the injuries depended on the voltage and amperage (amount of current). They say that the body's own resistance to the current plays a major role, as well as the current's path through the body, and how long the body remains in contact with the current. The severity of the injury is primarily determined by the amperage and not the voltage.

Hands are frequently involved in electrical injuries, as they are usually the most common initial source of contact with the electric current. Damage however, to other parts of the body are often more extensive and life threatening. It's clear from these journals that severe electrical shocks could result in cardiac arrest, fluid loss into swollen tissue and kidney failure. The kidney failure is a result of an overload of muscle protein from the damaged muscles.

The injuries occurred not only on the site of contact, but all along the path the electricity ran, as well as the exit location. Deep tissue injuries, caused by electrical shocks cause severe swelling that require deep incisions extending from hand to shoulder to relieve the pressure built up. If this is not done, the pressure caused by the swelling will shut off the blood supply to the affected area by compressing the arteries and resulting in further damage to the remaining tissue. The current therefore causes muscle, nerve and tissue destruction by passing through the body. Other factors determining the severity of the injuries would be the victim's own health and the adequacy and speed of the treatment received.

The flow of the current through the body could also result in severely burned internal organs and tissue as well as skin damage. In some cases, it can cause severe permanent neurological damage. Electrical shocks are also known for paralyzing the respiratory system or disrupt the rhythm of the heart, resulting in instantaneous death...

Electrical shocks cause death in 3% to 15% of cases. From the articles, many of the survivors require amputations as a result of the high-voltage injuries and in many cases, extensive skin grafts...

After the first few days spent in the Intensive Care Unit (ICU), our surgeon informed us that it was time for our first wound inspection. He was a bit concerned about blood flow to the healthy tissue. We actually thought that they were going to remove the bandages under sedation in theatre. When the surgeon however entered the ward with scissors, we knew it was going to happen there and then. He first removed the bandages from Niël's chest, revealing a clean, well stitched up incision where his left arm used to be. It looked a bit strange, as I was used to seeing an arm there, but in actual fact looked fine. He then removed the bandages from his legs, revealing severe burn wounds. He also removed the bandages from Hennie's body. Their injuries were very similar apart from Hennie's right arm having been amputated and neatly stitched up. Then it was my turn.

The doctor started removing the bandages around my chest. When the bandages felt stuck and he struggled getting them off, he seemed concerned and called for a nurse. A nurse arrived and gave me a morphine injection. According to the surgeon, that would help with the pain when removing the bandages. I could feel the bandages tearing my flesh and turned my head away from the wound. Looking at Niël's face when the doctor removed the last part of the bandages and dressing, I could tell that something seemed wrong. The doctor however, told me in a calm and well controlled voice that everything seemed to be in order. Although they had to remove all the skin from the amputation site, the blood was red and the drain pipes had done their job. He told me that a skin graft would have to be done at a later stage to cover the exposed area on my shoulder. Feeling nauseous after the experience, the surgeon continued to remove the bandages around the stump where my right leg used to be. Again he looked very impressed, and told me that they would soon begin to form the stump by way of stretch bandages to accommodate a prosthetis.

Next he started removing the bandages from my left foot, revealing a fresh wound where my toes had been. It actually appeared as if my toes had been axed off recently, or cut off by a sharp knife. It appeared gory and I was horrified! About half the skin of what was left of my foot was gone and would require extensive skin grafts. "How does it look?", he asked. I could not believe how calm he appeared, taking into account the severity of the injuries I had sustained. I couldn't answer. For the first time, we were really faced with the hard truth of the injuries we had sustained. I knew that this was the surgeon's way of bringing us back to reality, to enable us to get used to the idea of our lost limbs. It would help us accept our *new bodies*. Looking at the injuries, I knew that it could only get better from there.

Or could it?

ADAPTING TO NEW BODIES

AFTER A FEW more days in the ICU, we were transferred by ambulance to the orthopaedic section of HF Verwoerd Hospital. The three of us had our own private room, specifically designed for our needs. In the beginning, only close family members were allowed to visit, due to the constant threat of infection. Each of us underwent several skin graft operations. Hennie and Niël had skin grafting done to several open wounds on their legs and buttocks. I had skin grafts on my shoulder area and left foot. They used the healthy skin from the top of our thighs to cover the exposed areas. On the harvested areas thick scabs formed.

The skin grafts were successful and the harvested areas healed well, but initially left ugly scar tissue. The skin graft on my left foot was of some concern to the surgeon. One morning he instructed a nurse to remove the dead skin from my foot with tweezers after soaking my foot in water and *Betadine*. This ordeal lasted two gruelling hours. Two long hours of carefully removing dead tissue, piece by piece. This was an experience on its own as one could imagine.

The skin graft done on my shoulder healed well within a short period of time and the tiny stitches holding the skin together initially, were removed.

We were fortunate to have escaped the accident without any internal organ damage, and this brought some relief in coping with what we had lost.

Naturally, our parents and family were the first to visit us, later followed by our friends. Seeing our friends from school for the first time after the accident brought about a sense of discomfort and unease, but also a feeling of normality. "How would they react?" Previously a healthy and fit sportsman, now bed ridden. Many came to visit. There were many tear filled eyes but most left with a smile upon finding out that we were still the same friends they had known, even if physically different. It felt so strange having been *normal* prior to the holiday, and now, only a month later *different*. "How does one define normality?" I thought.

For the next two months or so, the hospital room became our second home. It became the place where each of us had to learn to accept our *new* bodies and determine the boundaries of our own individual inabilities and abilities. Assisted with help, understanding, love, affection and support from family, friends and hospital personnel, the road to recovery was a lot easier to endure. In the end though, the process of accepting one's body remains one's own. The fact that I was not alone in the situation also helped a lot. Our wounds were healing and that helped with regaining some mobility. I was soon able to hop out of the bed and into a wheelchair with the help of my brother or friend. I could explore the hospital surroundings and go outside to feel the warmth of the sun on my skin, which reminded me of all that life had to offer. Together with the healing of my wounds, came a spiritual and emotional healing. I remember the words of a poster against the wall in our hospital room:

"God, grant me the serenity to accept the things I cannot change, the courage to change the things I can, and the knowledge to know the difference."

It was time to learn about and minimize the physical limitations we were about to face in the world outside the hospital. We followed a strict routine consisting of occupational therapy and physiotherapy. The therapy helped us strengthen and improve muscle function and ability which had visibly deteriorated since our admission to the hospital. We now had to learn how to use only one hand in tasks that often required more than one. Occupational therapy, as part of the rehabilitation program, was necessary so as to enable us to combine skills with muscle function, in order to master daily routine tasks and more complex activities. Normal daily tasks like cutting bread or tying shoelaces became a challenge, and initially required the utmost patience to master.

Hennie and I also had to learn to write again, taking into account that we had both lost a right arm and had been right handed prior to the accident. This, on its own, required hours of practice and patience, so as to enable us to achieve that which becomes natural to most human beings after the first few years of primary school.

During our rehabilitation, I experienced a lot of divergent emotions, ranging from satisfaction when achieving a goal, to the deepest despair. Everything had now become a challenge.

We had to learn to adapt as soon as possible so that we would later be able to cope in the outside world. Life on the outside went on and here we were, on the side-lines for the moment.

During all these hospital activities, I was wheelchair bound, waiting for the stump to heal before I could be fitted with a prosthesis. Sometimes I had to rely on the assistance of nurses and other hospital personnel, which affected my independence. Although we received rehabilitation in a protected environment, we would soon realize the skills we had acquired in the hospital would become very significant in the world out there. Doing normal daily activities with only one arm, often required an active imagination to say the least.

The love, support and devotion from family and friends made the road to recovery a lot easier. Being alone in bed at night brought to mind fears and uncertainties on what the future would hold. These were the times I asked God to reveal some kind of answers to the questions lingering in my mind. And although I received no clear answers then, I knew that God had a plan with my life and would help me face my fears and resolve the uncertainties. Those quiet nights in the hospital also helped me put everything in perspective. Sometimes when looking at things from close by, you focus on the small things, and do not see the bigger picture. When looking at the bigger picture, it provides the situation with a different perspective. Listening to music through my earphones at night, I would often fall asleep with the soothing and comforting voice of Joni Eareckson Tada singing: "O Lord, please don't ever stop working with me, till you see, I can be, all you want me to be."

FACING CHANGES

ONE MORNING IN the hospital, approximately a month after the amputations, one of the nurses came into our room and informed me that the hospital's prosthetist was on his way to take the initial measurements for the stump on my right leg, in order to start the process of manufacturing my prosthesis. The laceration to the lower part of the stump had healed well with only a minor part of the soft tissue still swelled.

The previous night during wound inspection, the surgeon told me that I might have trouble balancing due to having lost both my right arm and right leg as well as the toes of my left foot. He also told me that I would most likely require a walking stick or crutch in addition to the prosthesis in the future to help me get around. His words caught me by surprise. Up until that moment, I had not doubted that I would be able to walk or even run without assistance. During our stay in the hospital, I received many visits from people wearing prosthetic limbs, assuring me that I would be able to return to a normal life without limitations when leaving the hospital. They had probably not taken into account that I had lost more than one limb, I thought. According to the doctor, the loss of toes always affects balance.

Before the accident, I was a healthy and fit athlete. Now I had to learn to walk again. I found it hard to accept. The idea of walking with a crutch or stick for the rest of my life... It dawned on me, that it would probably be only one of the many hurdles that I would have to face in the future. I would not give up. Whatever it took, I would walk unassisted one day.

Someone once said, "God chooses His bravest warriors for His greatest battles."

The prosthetist arrived dressed in a white jacket that reminded me of our dentist back home. He was a friendly guy and introduced himself to me while opening a box he had brought with him. I could see tools and screws inside, together with steel pipes and a strange looking rubber foot. With skill and determination he started drawing lines on the stump and took a few measurements. He opened bags containing plaster bandages. After pouring water into a plastic bowl, he soaked the plaster bandages in the water and skilfully began to wrap the stump with the bandages. When he was done, I could feel the heat on my skin building up inside the plaster dressing. It only took a few minutes for the plaster to set. He carefully removed the hard shell from the stump formed by the bandages. "Done," he said and began explaining the ins and outs of prosthetic limbs to me. How they fit. How they worked, and the materials they are made of. The shell formed by the plaster bandages would give him an exact imprint of the stump that would enable him to make a permanent socket out of fibre glass. That would then form the top part of the artificial leg. A pipe with a rubber foot on one end would then be attached to the socket. In my mind, I thought about how strange it would look to walk around on the pipe. He assured me as if he knew what I was thinking, that the most important thing about the leg would be functionality, and not the cosmetic side.

It was important to realize that the prosthesis would be able to stand in for many of the functions of the lost limb. Sometimes it is mainly cosmetic in nature, like in the case of an upper limb prosthesis. Even though some have a relatively good degree of functional capability. I had adapted well to doing things with only one hand, and I doubted whether I would really gain anything by getting an arm prosthesis... I was focused mainly on being able to walk again. The effective use of an artificial limb depended on the kind of amputation. The prosthetist explained that a person's age, build and state of health also played a role. He explained the balancing problems associated with an arm amputation, particularly when a large part of the limb was amputated.

I had many questions to ask. The prosthetist informed me that on occasion, complications did arise when using an artificial limb. Things like swelling of the stump, infection and friction could lead to blisters and skin rashes. Those were only rarely related to the materials used in the manufacturing of the prosthesis. Painful nerve swellings (neuroma) could develop on the stump, which would lead to further surgery. Following any of those complications, it would be necessary to go without the limb for a period of time, as continued use would lead to the condition worsening. I asked him about phantom pains I experienced. He explained that it was normal for a person to feel as if the limb was still there, and that it would occasionally be painful. The brain still sends signals to the part of the body that's absent. The pain would later on become merely a strange sensation...

The functional level achieved, he explained, would depend on a number of factors like age and the person's physical and mental state, as well as the level of amputation and construction of the stump. His motivation and the available rehabilitation programs are also important.

It took a considerable amount of time to process all the new information. It left me with a more optimistic attitude when the prosthetist left our room. I was extremely motivated to take on the new challenge with an *open heart* even with the strange thought of learning to walk again floating through my mind. The prosthetist would return later that week to fit the test socket. I would soon be able to walk again...

10

GOING OUT ON A LIMB

LATE ONE EVENING, my mother and I sat on my hospital bed discussing the possible balance problems the specialist had talked about. I told her that, although I had accepted the amputations, I still couldn't face life being handicapped and having to use a crutch to regain my mobility. After a moment of silence, she followed with a prayer asking for God's guidance through this problem. When she left, I felt peaceful knowing that my future was not in my hands and stared at the now well-known words on the wall in our room.

When the prosthetist returned later that week with my leg, I felt the uncertainness creeping up on me. The leg looked awkward and heavy and I wondered if I would ever overcome this hurdle. He gave me a woollen sock to pull over my stump before fitting the leg. The skin of the stump felt tender and painful inside the socket as I slowly lifted myself off the bed, carefully shifting my weight onto the prosthesis. Niël and Hennie looked astonished seeing me standing again after so many weeks. In the process of trying to move forward, I lost my balance and grabbed onto the railing of my bed. Everyone in the room was silent. All attention focused on me. The prosthetist, looking into my eyes could see the uncertainty. He calmly told me that I should take it slowly. Learning to walk again would take many hours of practise and patience...

Determined to walk again, I took the crutch in my arm. I shifted some of my weight onto the crutch, and slowly but surely, step by step, started moving forward. I felt dizzy with the blood pumping through my veins while standing but kept on going. When I reached the door to our room, I could hear the shouts of encouragement coming from Niël and Hennie. Although bursting with excitement, I had to keep my concentration on the task at hand, and I thought of Neil Armstrong's first words on the moon: "That's one small step for man, one giant leap for mankind." I was exhausted after about twenty meters down the corridor, and knew I had to rest and take it slowly. Although it felt uncomfortable walking with the heavy prosthesis strapped to my stump in the socket, I knew I would eventually get the hang of it. Standing on the prosthetic limb, I actually had the sensation of standing with both feet on the ground. This leg, however unfamiliar, would in the future become part of my anatomy. During the initial stages of walking, the idea of running again never crossed my mind. Learning to walk became my ultimate goal.

After I received my first prosthesis, I had to adapt to a different kind of rehabilitation from what I was used to. Now, as part of the walking nation once again, I had to learn how to regain balance and mobility. I had strict physiotherapy sessions where I had to regain muscle strength and flexibility in the remaining stump to be able to move around more freely. These sessions tested my patience to the extreme. Some days ended in despair, and others in pure glory. Learning not only to walk again, but how to walk again, had its own frustrations. The patience that the occupational therapist showed was astonishing. During those times, with my foot still bandaged and tender, I sometimes had to force myself to get up. With blood rushing to my injured foot the task ahead was just a bit more difficult. After many skin grafts, my foot was stitched up, but still swollen and tender. With no toes to propel me forward, I had to shift my balance onto the artificial leg to retain momentum.

Facing stairs had its own difficulties and presented new challenges. Climbing up required the constant shifting of weight between my legs. The normal thing to do would have been to always lead with the normal leg. The artificial leg would then simply follow, with constant pressure being put on the stronger leg.

Doing some investigations into momentum and stability in an amputee's gait, I discovered some worthwhile and informative information. A study was done on the turning gait of a trans-tibia amputee. Specialists then developed inventions that could increase functional mobility, safety and stability while turning. The inventions referred mainly to prosthetic inventions. The main focus point of these studies was to investigate how the properties of prosthetic components affect the gait of walking amputees. They indeed found that abnormal limb loading formed the principal factor in the occurrence of residual limp pain, which in turn caused instability and limited mobility. During the studies, they found that certain prosthetic components could improve the comfort, mobility and stability in more complex gait activities. Light weight prosthesis helped with some of the difficulties experienced.

During the previous decades, many studies were done on improving prosthetic components to improve the functionality of the prostheses and to enable the amputee to regain most of his mobility. The correct weight and fit was always important. There was a fine balance between having the prosthesis being neither too heavy nor too light. The strength of the components was also always a priority. Today though, there are thousands of components available, all with their own promise of returning, or improving mobility and delivering more energy for a better quality of live. Energy return became the focus point. The more energy created within an artificial limb, the better the forward propulsion.

Slowly but surely I learned to maintain my balance. The stump still got tender after a few minutes of walking, and sometimes the pressure of the socket around my knee became unbearable. Learning to walk again required perseverance and determination. I had to adapt to a world of artificial limbs, previously unknown to me. A world many people knew nothing about. Despite the agony I experienced the first few days after receiving the prosthesis, I was determined to walk again without the aid of the crutch, and this kept me motivated.

Roughly two weeks after I received the leg, I decided to try and balance without the crutch. I took the first two paces slowly but surely and was amazed by the fact that I was able to keep my balance. Overwhelmed by pure ecstasy, I kept on going down the corridor in the hospital ward. I suddenly realized that another miracle had happened. Despite the odds, I was able to walk on two legs again. When my parents came to visit, I shared the news with them. I could see the gratitude in my parents' eyes. I was on my way to recovery.

During our stay in the hospital, we received counselling from a psychologist as part of the rehabilitation program. After losing limbs, there are several stages a person has to go through to adapt and accept the facts, the psychologist explained. He told us that everyone had to set their own goals. The initial impossibilities would eventually become possible with a positive attitude and support from loved ones, coupled with determination to reach a specific goal. He told us that we would experience a lot of frustration and anger in the world outside the hospital. Society was often cruel and insensitive to other's feelings and needs.

We went to the prosthetist in the Louis Pasteur Building on many occasions to fit our artificial arms which we received a month after we'd been admitted to hospital. We had to leave the secure environment of the hospital, and were then exposed to the initial unaccustomed stares of members of the public. At the time I received my electric arm that had been imported from the USA, I had already adapted fairly well to doing everything with one hand and found the arm to be heavy and uncomfortable, and basically impractical. Although it appeared quite realistic cosmetically, I could not get used to the idea of something restricting my movement and mobility. I already had to learn to cope with one artificial limb, a leg I could not do without. The arm however, was a different matter and I later discarded it.

We were hospitalized for almost two months following the accident. During that time we came to terms with our new bodies and our own capabilities within a protected environment. In that protected environment we were constantly aware of the support and affection of the hospital staff, as well as family and friends. We knew that stage of our lives would also come to an end, and that we would have to face the outside world eventually. We were however, mentally and physically prepared for the challenge. I knew that there was still a reason for us being alive, and that we had to go out there and seek our destiny. As a fifteen year old boy, I was rather naïve and not yet fully equipped to realize the challenges that waited for me, but on the other hand it probably made my situation easier to accept.

The long road to recovery had begun...

11

FIRST GLANCE AT
THE OUTSIDE WORLD

O N 1 MARCH 1985 we received the welcoming news from the head
surgeon that we were being discharged. He was satisfied with our
progress and felt it was time for us to face the world out there, where
we would each learn our own limitations and capabilities. He could not
have chosen a better day. From the hospital our parents would drive us
to Pilditch stadium, a place well known to me, where our school was
competing in an inter-school athletics event.

Although very excited, it was also difficult and in a way sad to leave
our secure hospital room which had become our home for approximately
two months, the place where we laughed and cried; where we learned to
face and accept our situation. My heart was filled with gratitude towards
God. With the help of our families, we packed our bags in silence. We
then went to say goodbye to the devoted hospital staff who had played
such an important role in our recovery process. It was another emotional
experience and everyone was teary eyed when we left the hospital. This
was definitely the start of something new. We took a few photographs

outside the hospital before we left. This place had become our home for a short while and the memories of the experiences, both good and bad, would linger in our minds for many years to come.

On our way to Pilditch, I felt many emotions building up inside me, and touched the stump where my right leg used to be. "Previously a competitor, now a spectator" I thought. We decided it was best for me to attend the event in my wheelchair, knowing that I would not be able to endure a whole day of walking yet. I had to build up my strength again first. This made our entry into the stadium that much more difficult. I didn't want sympathy, or people feeling sorry for me. I had left school prior to the December holiday as an athlete and a sportsman, only to return *handicapped*. Oh, how I hated that word. And what does it really mean to be handicapped? I have some limitations, but so does everyone else. I decided never to consider myself handicapped. I would be victorious.

Upon entering the stadium, there was a festive feel to the air. Hundreds of school children were cheering and singing. I glanced at the track and saw a few athletes lining up for a sprinting event. Unwillingly, my thoughts went back a few months to when I was one of them. I remembered the sheer excitement and expectation when getting ready, doing those final stretch exercises before the event, the butterflies in the stomach, your heart pounding blood through your veins as you set your mind on the finishing line. I could still hear the shouts of encouragement from fellow school mates when lining up and weighing up the other competitors, and then the silence when kneeling down on the starting blocks, every muscle ready for the task ahead. Only you and the track in front of you. "Hi Braam!", I heard someone shout, bringing me back to reality in an instant. It was one of my close friends who saw me approaching in my wheelchair. Suddenly, the air erupted with shouts from other school mates on the pavilion while we approached. After a brief silence the whole school sang us a welcoming song.

A different kind of patience was needed to answer all the questions from our friends. Questions came from everywhere, all of them at once and assaulted our ears. It felt good to be back. Soon the heavy burden of sad emotions and thoughts were lifted from my mind. We had to repeat the entire story over and over again to satisfy our avid listeners. We'd returned, and we were once again part of *normal life*. Normal life that is such a blessing! We were welcomed back as heroes.

Exhausted, but thankful to have been able to join in the victory of our school that day, we left the stadium later that afternoon and headed home.

Being home brought many happy memories and a sense of well being. Still partially wheelchair bound, my dad had the great idea to build a ramp up the stairs in our house. I would then be able to manoeuvre myself from the living area to the bedrooms. Now fully wheelchair trained, I saw the ramp as a new and exciting challenge, and soon got the hang of it. It felt so good to be independent and in my own environment again.

The next day we had a wonderful get together with family and friends in our garden. We were happy to spend some quality time with close friends, and to have the time to share with them a bit of our experiences in the hospital. They in turn, had time to bring us up to date on the newest developments at our school. I knew that the sooner I got used to the prosthesis, the sooner I would be able to return to school. Returning to school would bring about another sense of normality! I never thought I would be able to miss school that much. With 80s music playing in the background, and the enthusiastic voices of family and friends just having fun, the day went by in a flash.

The following few days I spent many hours walking with my prosthesis, trying to get used to the constant pressure on the residual limb. During that time, I also had my first unpleasant experience with pressure sores. As explained to me by our doctor in the hospital, the skin of the residual limb in the socket first had to get use to the constant pressure applied by the weight of my body. Almost like wearing and walking in new shoes. Some of the pores could get blocked, resulting in infection. Due to constant pressure or friction in a certain area, the skin would react by forming pressure sores, further resulting in the tissue becoming even more infected and the tissue on the surface of the stump of the residual limb ultimately swelling.

When this happened, I had to wait for the swelling to subside before being able to put the leg on again, much to my frustration. The swelling is treated with antiseptic ointment and in severe cases with minor surgery. Wearing the leg while having pressure sores often worsens the situation and causes an even more severe infection, not to mention excruciating pain. During those times many amputees will be on crutches for a while, waiting for the infected area to heal before putting on the prosthesis again. Because I have also lost an arm, the crutch alternative was not an option for me. I only had two choices; either walk with the pressure sores, or be wheelchair bound for that period, which would be a few days.

I soon learned how to do the surgery myself with a local anaesthetic and scalpel to release the pressure. I would not recommend it to those who are squeamish. It took me quite some time to get the hang of it. After draining the pressure sore the pain would lessen. I could then easily put my leg on again.

While recuperating at home, I learned to ride my bicycle again. I used my left hand, with both the front and rear brake levers attached to the left side of the handlebar. It took some time getting used to it. Soon though, I was able to keep my balance on the bicycle and the rest came instinctively. Once again, I had my own wheels. Anything is possible if you apply yourself.

12

BACK TO SCHOOL

O N 20 APRIL 1985 it was time for us to go back to school again. We'd been absent for approximately two and a half months.

It was time for me to catch up on Grade 10.

During our stay in the hospital, we attended hospital school. The hospital teachers came to our room and we were kept up to date with the latest syllabus. Taking into account the physical state we were in, it was very difficult to concentrate on school work when everyone's main concern was recuperation and regaining muscle strength and mobility. Some of our friends and fellow pupils however, kept our schoolwork up to date, but we still had a lot of catching up to do.

Going back to school felt good. Like all the other pupils, we attended classes as normal. It would help us adjust easier when going into the open labour market, or if we chose to further our educations. The accident itself caused some interruption in my life. That interruption gave me ample opportunity to weigh future career possibilities...

Only time would tell what obstacles I had to face in order to follow my dreams.

Riding to school on my bicycle, with a heart full of gratitude, the already short distance to the gate felt even shorter than before, maybe too short. I learned to appreciate life and all it has to offer anew. Even going to school, previously only a part of my daily routine, felt different now. In a way, I felt whole again. Riding through the gate I noticed the amazed stares in the eyes of fellow pupils. When I reached the school building I received a warm welcome from my friends. Barely noticing my loss, they greeted me with their left hands. Wearing long trousers hid the leg prosthesis, and gave me an initial sense of security. I didn't want anyone making a fuss about it. I was still the same person. Being back at school and attending classes with my friends, I soon felt at ease and relaxed. I was one of them again.

I soon realized how much work I had missed being absent during the first semester. I would have to work hard to catch up again. I did not want to be left behind. I had to carry my school case myself, and would not be excused if I arrived late for any class. I had to abide by the rules like everyone else. Being back at school helped a lot with adapting to my circumstances and exploring the limits of my abilities.

To improve muscle strength and tone I joined a local gym. There I was able to push my boundaries, which helped a lot with regaining self-confidence. Being a sportsman prior to the accident, I was used to training hard and I soon found out that many of the exercises helped me to improve my mobility and balance. After going to the gym, I would take a long swim in our pool at home, relaxing tired and strained muscles. For a leg amputee, daily exercise like walking and climbing stairs can be a strenuous activity. In order to obtain maximum mobility, my left leg and arm took most of the strain, sometimes resulting in neck and back pain. I was coping well without the toes on my left foot, walking over the top to propel me forward. The skin on the front part of my foot became hard as the sole itself.

Some activities took quite a while to master, like tying shoelaces one handed and cutting bread. After school, my brother and I had to make our own lunches. With only two arms between the two of us, it went quite slowly in the beginning. We soon learned to do some of the tasks together when preparing food. Opening a can was a problem all on its own, but when you have to, you make a plan. As the old saying goes: "Where there's a will, there's a way." In a way, I had no option but to adapt in order to survive, literally, when preparing food. To peel a potato or slice a tomato was another challenge. When you have all your limbs intact, one seldom thinks about the way you do daily tasks, as everything comes naturally. I learned to appreciate the fact that I still had one hand which enabled me to retain my independence.

In the evenings I relaxed in front of the television with my family after finishing my homework. My writing was still much slower than what it had been before the accident, making notes in class therefore much more difficult. Sometimes I even had to decipher my own handwriting after class, just to make sense of what I had written.

While in the hospital, everyone helped us with daily tasks. Now I had to work out a plan myself to adjust to circumstances. When dining out, I usually accepted the waitress's offer to help me cut my steak, which she did with the utmost precision, much to the amusement of my family.

Throughout our recovery period, humour played a significant role in helping us come to grips with our situation. For school, I tucked the right sleeve of my jacket into the right hand pocket. Many of my friends used this as an opportunity to playfully tease me, saying that according to the school rules, we were not supposed to walk around with our hands in our pockets.

As the days went by, I silently longed to be back on the beach in Buffalo Bay. Our previous holiday had been cut short by an event beyond our control, a freak accident. The fact that we'd survived the ordeal could only be described as a miracle. Many of the surgeons in the hospital told us that from the evidence we had most certainly received a second chance in life. The mere fact that none of us had suffered cardiac arrest or any other kind of internal organ damage as a result of the 11 000 volts shock, could not be explained by medical personnel. Knowing God still had a reason for me to be on this earth filled me with gratitude and a hunger for life. The accident itself brought about stronger family bonds, much stronger than before.

We planned to return to our beloved Buffalo Bay at the end of the year to enjoy another summer vacation. I could not wait to go back there. The previous time we had left in such a hurry under extreme circumstances. But before then, I first had to pass my year-end exams.

In June of 1985 we also had the privilege of going to Swaziland for a short family vacation. Between the beautiful green mountains and crisp air of the Ezulwini valley, (Place of heaven), I had the chance to recharge my batteries for the final stretch to the end of the year. During our stay in the hospital, we'd been followed around by a filming crew to record our recovery for a documentary, entitled *Appointment at the seaside*. The members of the team accompanied us to Swaziland to continue filming in the tranquil environment. This came with some level of exposure. While being recorded, I experienced the freedom of swimming weightlessly in the hotel pool, despite the captivated stares of onlookers. Being used to the constant camera attention by now, I found the growing interest in our whereabouts kind of addictive. The cameras helped a lot with getting used to the unfamiliar attention. I did not feel uncomfortable with my appearance at all, but rather experienced a sense of freedom in being able to express myself in public. I made peace with the fact that, for the rest of my life, I would be the centre of attention in any public place.

The surroundings of the beautiful countryside with its vast open spaces and friendly people overwhelmed me and ensnared my inner being, in a way that's difficult to express. I fell in love with Swaziland and its people. We went for long walks through dense indigenous forests, the constant soothing sound of waterfalls gurgling filling the air. Here I experienced a freedom of living I had never experienced before. The constant throbbing pain, caused by my new prosthesis digging into my flesh had no effect on the abundance of life I felt walking through the forests. The blisters I would treat later that evening. The constant presence of the cameras also helped me maintain my posture throughout the day. Afterwards, we went for a relaxing neck and back massage at one of the local spas. This place was what I imagined heaven to be.

Whether walking, eating or sleeping, the constant presence of the camera was there, capturing my every move. The film crew later on became like family to us, always present. We knew that this documentary could give hope to those in despair. It would also help uplift the minds of those feeling that life had become too much to endure. In a way, I also felt grateful for being used as a medium through which others could be given hope in their time of need, showing them what life had to offer despite any setbacks they might have experienced. The trip to Swaziland was definitely worthwhile.

Back in Pretoria I received the unexpected news that I had been chosen as one of a few recipients of the Prudential, *Sunday Times* "Youth Bravery Award", presented by former State President P.W. Botha's wife, Ms Elize Botha. During the event I had the privilege to meet many of the heroes from the Westdene bus disaster. The event was held in Johannesburg as a salute to acts of valour performed by South Africa's youth. I will never forget Ms Elize Botha's words in her opening speech:

> "Bravery is not an act of foolhardy or reckless behaviour, it is
> behaviour that combines a measure of confidence with caution,
> in a way that requires some forethought and a genuine concern

for danger. This does not mean that the life of a brave person isn't sometimes tragically lost by performing an act of bravery."
During the event, I shared in the emotional and heartwarming stories of the other recipients, and empathised with their inner pain. I was also interviewed for a youth program which was aired on national TV. We enjoyed a lovely three course dinner in the presence of famous people. Afterwards I went to my luxury hotel room reserved for the event. Grateful to have spent a great evening with my parents, I fell asleep in my hotel bed dreaming of what had yet to come.

13

FUTURE DREAMS

ALTHOUGH NOT THE most dedicated of readers, during my recovery time I did read a few motivational and inspirational books, given to me as presents by loved ones. One of the books that was titled "Reach for the Sky", tells the story of Douglas Bader. He was believed to be Britain's most courageous fighter pilot. It is the story of a man who lost both his legs in battle and his ability to conquer disability. In many ways, I could relate to his story and found the book difficult to put down. Douglas Bader had to learn to walk with legs made out of leather and metal. Against all odds though he gained the respect of many, not only by learning to walk again, but in returning as a fighter pilot and golf player. A truly uplifting story.

As an adrenalin junkie and inspired by the fact that many of my friends had motorcycles, I thought about the possibility of riding a motorcycle with one arm. My parents disapproved of motorcycles before the accident because of the risks involved. I knew it would take a lot of convincing to persuade them now. Riding a bicycle just wasn't as much fun as before, and being a passenger on the back of my friend's motorcycle was not enough either. I wanted to be in control of one of those machines. I had never seen someone riding a motorcycle with only one arm before. Nothing is impossible though. Much to my surprise while paging through a magazine, I found an article about a guy from Johannesburg riding his Kawasaki Ninja with only his left arm. He had lost his other arm in a motor vehicle accident. "Is this a sign or what?", I thought. Not exactly sure how to approach my parents with the idea, I at least knew that it was possible to ride a motorcycle with one arm. If he could do it, so could I!

Armed with the magazine article and enough courage to take on an army, I approached my parents using an emotional tactic, telling them how uncomfortable it was riding my bicycle with the prosthesis. It was the truth. Being on a motorcycle, I would be able to travel more easily without having to think about my prosthesis. From their faces, I could see that they were not taken with the idea. The magazine article didn't help much.

Strangely enough, it was my dad who brought my attention to an advertisement in the newspaper about a second hand motorcycle that was for sale, possibly because he'd owned a motorcycle when at university. The following evening we went to have a look at the motorcycle, and although not the prettiest of motorcycles, purchased it immediately. My friend rode the motorcycle back home, where it stood for two days before my dad had the time to make the necessary modifications. We moved the throttle and the front brake lever over to the left hand side so I would be able to ride the motorcycle with one hand. I soon became accustomed to the conversion and began riding the motorcycle to school, much to the astonishment of my friends. Riding the motorcycle, I had to keep my concentration on the task at hand and not get confused with the levers. I did have a spectacular fall once when a dog decided to cross the road in front of my motorcycle on a wet rainy day. Fortunately, I sustained only a few cuts and bruises, the worst being a bruised ego, because of falling in front of the drum majorettes. I soon got the hang of the controls.

I joined my friends riding around and going to gym. Riding the motorcycle gave me an entirely new sense of freedom.

When the time arrived for me to go for my driver's license, my mother made the appointment. I passed the learner's test easily enough and only had to go back for the road test. Completing the road test without any mistakes earned me my license. Being a legal road user contributed to my sense of achievement and made me more confident in my riding skills. My mom and I had an agreement that I would keep the motorcycle until I was old enough to drive a car. I would then sell the motorcycle in favour off a car. The agreement seemed fair and left me with at least another two years of riding.

At school I tried to participate in all the events that was possible for me to participate in. Playing football with the other boys was fun. Once I got too enthusiastic though, and when I kicked the soccer ball with all my strength and might, my leg came off. I'll never forget the look on my friend's face, filled with awe and shock when the ball and leg reached him simultaneously, leaving me to hop along on one leg...

My brother and I received a table tennis table as a gift from a chain of supermarkets. Playing table tennis definitely improved our hand-eye coordination, especially mine, with having to switch over to the left hand.

Although rather busy with extra curricular activities, I would often make time to watch the athletes practicing after school on the track. Sitting on my motorcycle, I would dream of the days when I had competed. Being a spectator in life was boring to say the least. I didn't even know any of the words to the songs they sang, because I had always participated in the sports. I missed the roaring of the crowd in my ears while on the track. I silently wondered if I would ever be able to compete again. Academically, I did OK, but sports were my terrain. Something about practicing was addictive and helped me to focus on my life forward. I knew that taking into account the fact God gave me a talent for sport, I would eventually be able to participate in some kind of competitive sport again. I missed being a member of a team. Playing rugby had given me so many close friendships in the past. To be a team member is certainly something everyone desires. Both making friends and playing a crucial role in the success of the game added to a sense of worthiness. Although not being able to do hurdles any longer, my former athlete friends still supported me. It made me realize that life itself does not consist of sport alone, but of a complex interaction between it and other activities, relationships and personalities; thus binding us together, making us human beings. As a spectator, there is also the advantage of meeting and interacting with people who I would previously never have had the time or opportunity to meet. Not everyone has the ability or talent to participate in sports, but they may excel in other aspects of life. Maybe God opened some doors for me while closing others. I still needed to find the boundaries of my existence. With one arm, I had the privilege of embracing more people than when I had two before the accident.

14

WOLRAAD

IN SEPTEMBER 1985 my mother gave me a letter that came through the post. It was a letter from the office of the State President addressed to me. Anxiously, I tore open the envelope and started reading the first paragraph of the letter…

"It is our great pleasure to inform you that you have been chosen by the State President to receive the gold *Woltemade Decoration For Bravery*, in recognition of the outstanding bravery shown in the most extreme and life threatening situation on 26 December 1984, when you saved your brother's life."

Astonished by the words, I had to reread the first paragraph again to make sense of it. I had never thought of myself as a hero. I had done what I had to do under the circumstances. I did what anyone else would do if their brother or sister's life were in danger. How does one define a hero?

The occasion would be held on 9 November 1985 at the Presidential Guest House (Old Presidency) in Pretoria. Dark suits for the men and dresses with hats for the ladies as dress code. The letter also requested that I confirm whether or not I would accept the decoration for bravery. The Woltemade Decoration was instituted in 1970 as the highest decoration for bravery to be awarded to citizens of South Africa performing extraordinary deeds of bravery in the face of death. Only eleven of these medals had previously been handed out. The letter was signed by the Secretary General to the State President, Mr. P.W. Botha.

My parents helped me write a formal letter of acceptance.

As part of the invitation I was allowed four guests that could accompany me to the occasion. Naturally, my family would go with me.

On 9 November 1985 we arrived at the home of the State President in my dad's car. The enormous gates leading to the house were opened by the State President's guards. I was very excited at being able to meet the State President in person. Driving down the long driveway between old oak trees towards the house, I could feel the anticipation building up in every inch of my body. I felt honoured and privileged for receiving this decoration. How could anyone compare me saving my brother to the deeds of the great and well known hero Wolraad Woltemade? He saved fourteen people from the sinking ship, "De Jonge Thomas", on the back of his horse before himself drowning as a result of exhaustion. What I did in a matter of seconds on that dreadful day, I did instinctively without thinking about my own safety. Despite the fact that I lost limbs, I would do the same again a thousand times over despite the consequences. How can you weigh up your own safety against the life of loved one?

To experience the event with my whole family gave me a considerable amount of joy and gratitude. Not only did I still have a brother, but also a fellow survivor. No one would know what the outcome could have been on that day if I had not turned around. Our second life started on 26 December 1984. In future, that day would be commemorated the same way as a birthday, a second chance in life.

Entering the big homestead, I felt overwhelmed by the vast open spaces of the glamorous building. We received a friendly welcome from staff members and were shown to our seats amongst the other recipients and guests. Everything was very formal, but spectacular too. We sat in silence as the President addressed the guests with an opening speech. A few months ago, I would have never envisaged myself in such a situation.

Shaking the President's hand was a moment in my life that I would never forget. I would also remember the constant flashing of cameras from the press when President Botha awarded me the Medal for Bravery. I was one of eight to receive the decoration in gold that year. Three of the eight recipients received the decoration posthumously. Twenty two recipients received the decoration in silver.

Afterwards there was a lovely lunch in the garden and I spent some time with the other recipients, most of whom I had previously met at the Youth Bravery Awards. They were heroes from the Westdene bus disaster. Talking to them I could still feel and see in their eyes the grief and sorrow they had experienced from the loss of their friends. In a way we shared the same thing, a second chance in life.

It was a moment in time I would cherish for the rest of my life. After an eventful day, I could only thank God for keeping us together and assisting us in making the right choices when the need arose. Surely our lives were not in our own hands. Surely our deeds were governed from above? My heart was filled with gratitude as I sat in the back of my dad's car while he drove us home through the streets of Pretoria.

At school, some of my friends started calling me *Wolraad* while others called me *The One Armed Bandit* for some or other reason. Now it was time to focus on the coming year-end exams. I had been able to catch up with most of the work lost during my stay in the hospital. The year ahead could only bring more opportunities. So many things had happened since our discharge from the hospital, but finally it felt as if life had eased back into normality.

BACK AT LAST

FEELING THE COOL breeze from the sea on my face, I was overwhelmed with joy. It had been almost a year after the accident and so many things had happened in between. The older I became, the quicker the years seemed to fly by. It was like yesterday that we planned the sailing trip from this specific spot. Looking back, I could only lift my arm in praise and thankfulness for the way in which God had guided me through the *Valley of Death*. Being able to stand here as a normal person, smelling the salty air and feeling the sun on my skin, was a true miracle. How I had longed to be here again and suddenly my wish had come true.

We so easily use the words, "Let Your will be done", in prayer, without actually realizing the consequences thereof. Sometimes in life, God allows bad things to happen to His children so that He can mould us for a higher spiritual purpose. Having been moulded made me feel special in a way that words cannot describe. I had started trusting Him from very early in my life, knowing not to expect a clearly defined answer to every question I had. Quite clearly, God had a plan for my life.

During the past year there had been many moments in which I felt anger towards God. I could not understand how He could have allowed the accident when He had given me a talent for sport. It was most certainly not something I deserved!

I remembered praying to God many times at night to just give me back my toes. It would make walking so much easier and I could live with the loss of my arm and leg. How I would love to be able to walk barefoot on the sand again, digging my toes into the wet sand.

Remember though that God is the miracle worker, through Him **nothing** is impossible! Sometimes we must accept NO as an answer. It took a while for me to really accept my loss and turn it into an opportunity. Many questions remained unanswered when looking back at the accident and the consequences thereof through the eyes of a mere human. Having to walk with the pain of pressure sores made me even angrier with God. Some of my questions would remain unanswered on this earth, but I found joy in accepting who I am and decided to make the best of every opportunity that came my way. I've come to learn that other people won't accept me before I accept myself the way I am. Looking at my reflection in a mirror shortly after the accident was tough. I had to relearn to love what I see. Looking in a mirror today however, I see a whole person. I love what I see because God loves me. This fight was not only a physical one, but also a mental, spiritual and emotional battle.

God knows the best for us… We have to trust in Him as children do.

For our summer holiday in 1985 we all decided to go back to Swartvlei at *Bleshoender Station* to sail with our friends on their new catamaran, so that we could finish what we had started. It would bring some closure. We would wait for the right opportunity and weather. The sailing expedition would also form part of the last scenes of the documentary, "Afspraak By Die See (Appointment by the seaside)."

Arriving at the coast, there were a lot of uncertainties and insecurities in my mind as to how people would react seeing me on the beach again. I would hate it if people were to feel sorry for me or react too compassionate. I had had time to come to grips with my situation and felt at ease with myself.

On the beach, doctors, engineers, managing directors, professors and school teachers are stripped of their titles and appear in their best bathing suits when in the public eye. On the beach the differences between people are minimalized. They embrace being *tourists* and the normal public divisions between people are non-existent. Everyone is there with one purpose – to relax. That in itself, made the situation more bearable. I would have liked to blend in with the crowds. Unfortunately, that didn't happen. Arriving at the beach, I took off my shirt and I could immediately feel the staring eyes of everyone on the beach. I had suddenly become the main attraction. "Had none of these people ever seen an amputee before?", I thought. A year ago I had gone unnoticed... Suddenly, now all the attention was focused on me. It took a while to get used to that, but after some time I just took it in my stride.

There is a lesson in life to learn from this. We, as Christians, sometimes only want to blend in. It is difficult at times to stand up for what we believe in and by making a stand, we often attract attention. That attention isn't always pleasant to endure but as Christians we have to take this stand to proclaim what we believe in.

I took my body board and fins, as well as my wetsuit to the beach. I wanted to take on the waves again as soon as possible. Dressed in my wetsuit, it was easier to blend in and I took my board and headed for the waves. Going through the first line of breakers, I suddenly felt at home in the water again. I paddled to the last line of surfers waiting for the waves to form. Paddling with one arm and kicking with one leg was something to get used to. Although not as agile as before, I was coping. That day the waves were larger than I was used to. A strong breeze was blowing from the land, forming waves with perfect white crests.

The first wave coming in hit me unexpectedly while I was turning around. I could feel the strength of the ocean against my body. In the process of trying to stay afloat, I felt the wave tearing away my body board. The leach around my arm that connected me to my board snapped as a result of the powerful wave and the board was snatched from my arm. In the process, I could also feel the power of the surge as it pulled on my prosthesis and I realized that it had come loose. I shouted to a surfer going by for help and he approached me on his surfboard. "I lost my leg!" The words slipped out. The surfer, unaware of what had really happened, looked around terrified in the murky water for sharks. It took me quite a while to reassure him and explain what had actually happened. He then went to fetch my leg, which was floating on the surface and brought it back to me. Walking out onto the beach, I had a smile of relief on my face. "What else would I have to endure?", I thought. During the next few days, I got accustomed to the waves and spent hours riding the big waves with the locals.

Our film team thought footage of the three of us water skiing together again would be great. I hadn't given this possibility a thought. "Would I be able to hold onto the rope?" "Would my prosthetic leg be able to endure the pressure while skiing?" "It's worth a try," I thought...

Nothing is impossible. As luck would have it, we met an old school friend whose dad owned a ski boat; we finalised the plans and everything was set. We would try the impossible.

When I gave the signal, I could hear the engines of the boat roar in acceleration. In a matter of seconds, after feeling as if my arm would be torn from my body, I was pulled out of the water and hung on to the rope with all my strength. To my astonishment, I was afloat with walls of white foam coming from the skis. I was really doing it. Gliding swiftly over the water. Almost floating on air, I felt a new sense of freedom. Amazed by the possibilities, I knew nothing on earth would ever keep me from trying the seemingly impossible again.

It was a year after the accident and our plans for sailing again fell into place. The weather was perfect. We were going to the same spot where we had been a year ago. Reaching our destination, we were silent, each one lost in his own thoughts. Everything seemed so quiet and peaceful. No one would ever have imagined the tragedy which had unfolded here a year ago. The power lines, running between pine poles, seemed so harmless now, bearing enough electricity to power a town. Would the outcome have been different if the deadly power lines had been more visible on that cloudy day, I wondered? Without regrets and overwhelmed by the opportunity for which we had waited many months, we started getting the boat ready for sailing. Now, fully aware of the danger lurking, we rigged the yacht close to the water. Unlike the previous time when there had been so many other people around, there was nobody else that day. In that specific spot a life changing accident had happened only a year ago, I thought. From where I was standing, I could now clearly see the warning sign erected after the accident, with the words:

DANGER!
HIGH-VOLTAGE
OVERHEAD POWERLINES
GEVAAR!
OORHOOFSE HOOGSPANNINGSDRADE.

When we were once again on the water, on the yacht and sailing, all negative thoughts were gone from my mind. Now it was time to finish what we had started a year ago. With the wind jerking on the sails and the air filled with the excited voices of my brother and friends, it was a moment I would never forget. We had fulfilled what we came to do. We were once again, young boys enjoying and making the best of what nature had to offer: Boys who had had to learn to be men, probably too early in their lives.

16

GOING FOR GREEN

A MUTUAL FRIEND introduced us to sports for the disabled, although I didn't much like the word *disabled*, never before having thought of myself as such. I would soon realize though that this opportunity would definitely be more than just being a part of another rehabilitation program. We soon found out that there was a professional organization specializing in promoting sport for the disabled on a highly competitive basis. Athletes from around the country would come together to be classified according to his or her own degree of disability by a panel of doctors. This enabled each one to participate in a category suited to them against other athletes with similar disabilities.

I originally focused on field events like javelin, shot-put and discus throwing. Having never before been a field athlete, it took a considerable amount of time and effort to learn the correct techniques. I spent hours practicing on any open field available, the whole time improving on my distances. Although now fully adapted to using my left hand, participating in an event like javelin initially felt quite uncomfortable with the left arm, as I had been right handed before the accident. When we held our first athletics meeting I was confident that I would perform well within my category. Unfortunately, there were no other participants in my category attending the meeting, and I had to compete against myself; trying to reach distances previously set by other athletes in the same category. I soon surpassed the distances set down as the South African records in these events. I received my Northern Transvaal colours and became the new South African Champion in my category. Unfortunately, without any fierce competition I soon lost interest in these field events as a result of competing against myself and setting my own new records.

As a competitive athlete, I decided that I had to learn to run again. At that time, I had a moderate to high activity level prosthesis, which would enable me to run again. That which had come naturally, now became a new challenge. Starting in our garden with my old spikes on both feet I slowly learned to build up speed again, putting my trust in the strength and assembly of the prosthesis and shifting my weight evenly between both my legs. Deteriorated and little used muscle had to be built up again and then stretched and exercised.

My prosthesis had a leather strap attached to the socket, which I fastened around my knee to give me better security. Learning to run was like learning to walk again after the accident. It took a lot of determination and pain which eventually paid off. An artificial leg will never truly substitute a real leg, with muscles and tendons all working together to give a fluid motion when running or walking. Carbon fibre, fiberglass, nuts and bolts now had to simulate that natural fluidity. The secret in the performance and comfort of the prosthesis is not only in the quality of the material used in the manufacturing process, but in the way the socket fits around the residual limb. Different feet also create different levels of energy return. Almost like wearing new shoes. An ill-fitting socket will cause blisters more easily than one with a perfect fit. I am sure any prosthetist would agree that the secret lies in manufacturing a socket that resembles as closely as possible the normal contours of the remaining bones and tendons on the residual limb. In a way, forming a second skin over the residual limb with no airflow in-between; also called a close-fitting prosthesis. I initially and incorrectly believed that the more you walk on the leg the less the pain will become.

A further crucial aspect of the performance of the prosthesis lies in the correct alignment. Incorrect alignment may cause further imbalance and mobility difficulties, which in itself could result in incorrect posture, walking or running style. It took quite a while for me to establish the correct alignment to be able to run. The alignment is also influenced by the way in which your other leg performs and moves. Every amputee therefore has a different degree of alignment to resemble the other leg's movement. Alignment in my case, was made even worse by the fact that I had no toes on my left foot to propel me forward. I eventually established a running style that suited me and took into account my specific needs. At the next athletics meeting, I signed up as a sprinter.

Before I could compete as a track athlete however, I had to qualify for the South African Championships that were to be held later that year in Port Elizabeth. Confident in my abilities, and with many hours of gruelling practice behind me, I arrived at the Northern Transvaal Championships held in Pretoria. I was amazed to see and meet so many other leg amputees who attended this meeting for the same purpose. To be the best and to qualify...

To my disappointment, I again had no competitors in my specific category, considering that I had lost an arm as well. Nonetheless, I decided to give it my best in order to qualify for the Championships. For practical reasons as well as to encourage competitiveness the sponsors decided to let all the leg amputees compete in the same race. Each one striving to reach their own qualifying time. Before the race, I got the same feeling of anticipation I had experienced so many times before in my life as a track athlete. With my heart pounding in my chest, I kneeled down and waited for the shot from the starter. All went well and I finished the race within the time limit. And although I qualified and obtained my Northern Transvaal colours in the 100 and 200 meters, I realized that there was much room for improvement. My time in the 100 meters was around 15 seconds. When I received my medal, I felt a warm sense of pride and achievement, realizing that hours of practice had eventually paid off.

During this time I met an older guy named Willie, with a below the knee amputation. He became my idol and mentor. He ran competitively and had managed to complete the Comrades Marathon with a carbon fibre running blade prosthesis. It was the first one I had ever seen. Willie knew what running was all about and ran effortlessly around the track.

Later that year, we drove down to Port Elizabeth in Niël's car for the South African Championships. With a backup leg in the boot of the car, in the unfortunate event of the other one delaminating, we made our way down to the coast. We were filled with excitement over the coming Championships. Not only would this meeting be a test of our strength and endurance, but also a time to meet up with many of the people we had met through participating in athletics for the disabled, many of whom had endured far worse experiences in life than we had. Some of the most competitive athletes were in wheelchairs, certainly an inspiration to all. Sports for the disabled, unlike popular belief, requires even more determination than for those athletes without a handicap. "These are the real heroes!" I felt proud being a part of this special group of people, knowing and experiencing the way they had learned to overcome their hardships and living life to the fullest. They are real people. None of them see themselves as *disabled*, but more as *physically challenged*. Off the track, they would make fun of their circumstances with loads of humour. But when it came to competing, the concentration and determination was fierce. These guys were the real athletes!

Before I could compete in the final, I first had to qualify in the elimination rounds. I qualified for the finals in both the 100 and 200 meters, and had a few days to rest before the final events. The strong wind, high temperatures and humidity along this part of the coast also took its toll and tested one's endurance and fitness level.

In the evenings we went into town to dine and relax aching and strained muscles. We spent some time on the beach and savoured the last few hours of the day when the sun threw its orange blanket over the sea, just before darkness fell…

Too soon the time for the final event arrived. Still not having a fellow competitor in the 200 meter event, I would again be competing against the clock. For this event, I decided to leave the leather strap unbuckled, giving me more freedom of movement in my stride. After a warm up session, I confidently walked back to the starting point. The spectators fell silent when I kneeled down at the starting line. The shot went off. In the first 100 meters everything went quite well, and I knew I was running a record breaking time. And because it was my final race at the Championships, it made me push even harder than before. I was breathing fast and my throat burned from the exertion. Then it happened! I could feel my prosthesis slowly coming loose. In my mind though I knew I had to finish the race and keep running. There was no time for hesitation or slowing down. I had to keep my stride. But with every stride the situation became worse. When I was about 10 meters from the finishing line, my prosthesis suddenly came off and I hit the tartan with full force. I could hear the encouraging shouts from the spectators echoing in my ears. When I realized what had happened, I instinctively knew I had to finish the race. I crawled the last few meters over the finishing line and finished well out of the time limit but still got the medal. "At least I finished the race," I thought.

Sometimes in life we fall. It's not the fall that counts but getting up and going on that matters.

In 2001 I had the privilege of participating in the ABSA relay. I received an invitation for this worthy cause a few weeks prior to the event and was happy to accept. It was a prestigious event held annually to encourage employees from many different firms to participate. My team consisted of Niël, other amputees as well as celebrities like Callie Strydom. Our aim was to raise funds for a child amputee. The funds would buy her an artificial leg.

I would be required to run approximately 2.5 kilometres in my section of the race. I was a bit hesitant due to being unfit and without a proper running leg. Al my doubts evaporated though when Willie, one of the other participants, offered to lend me one of his running legs for the event. It was a proper carbon fibre blade called a *C Sprint* that was specifically developed for long distance running. I would attach it to one of my own custom made sockets. I grabbed his offer without hesitation and accepted the invitation to be part of this memorable event.

Learning to run with the leg was a totally new experience. The energy return in the carbon blade was astonishing, compared to the previous legs I had run with. For the same reason, walking with this leg was almost impossible. The leg required drastic forward motion in order to achieve the full benefit and energy return from the strong, but flexible and almost indestructible carbon blade. It took me a while to get used to the feeling of the leg before I could think of running with it. I had a custom fit silicone sleeve made to wear with the prosthesis with a full contact socket. Another silicone sleeve would be used over my socket to keep the air out, causing a suction effect. The socket itself felt very soft and comfortable around my knee joint but the pressure on the residual limb caused by the close fitting socket was definitely something to get used to. The leg definitely felt more secure as a result of the suction effect.

I started practicing, at first running around the block in the vicinity of our home. Running became a bit easier every day and I soon felt confident on the carbon blade. I had to put my trust in the strength and manufacturing of the blade. Going shopping with the leg after practicing drew a lot of attention from the public. It didn't bother me in the least however. In a way, it felt nice being different and receiving stares of disbelief.

The event was held in Johannesburg and we left Pretoria early that Sunday morning to be in time to get to our different starting points. Reaching my starting point, I knew that much depended on my performance that day. Although my section of the race was the shortest, if I failed to reach the next point, the whole race would be disrupted. It made me feel quite important, like a crucial link in the chain, and as a member of the running team with a specific goal in mind.

Stretching and warming up, waiting for the member of our team of the previous section to arrive, I could see disbelief and admiration on the faces of other participants running this section of the race with me. When our team member handed me the relay baton, I started off at a quick pace, nearly running over a photographer who appeared in my path taking photographs. During the race, I constantly received words of encouragement from runners passing me by as well as from spectators along the route. It was warm and the salt from the sweat running down my face blurred my vision, but I kept on going. When I reached the end of my section I could see Niël waiting for me, standing between the roaring crowds of spectators. Exhausted but relieved, I handed him the relay baton. Trying to catch my breath after the race, I felt proud that I had been able to complete the race and contribute to a worthy cause. We succeeded in our goal and made a difference in a child's life...

LEGAL EAGLE

WHEN I WAS still a boy, I dreamt of becoming a doctor or a dentist, just like two of my uncles. I also thought of a career as a veterinary surgeon because of my love for animals. I had always been drawn to the medical profession from an early age, wishing to one day make a difference in someone else's life. It was to my mind, a respectable profession.

As I grew older, the idea of being qualified in the medical profession persisted and in 1986 I went for aptitude tests. It was clear from the tests that my interests lay in the medical and law fields working with people. After the accident in 1984, my scope narrowed somewhat. I wanted to be in a profession where I would be equal to my fellow students on both an academic and physical level. I had to accept that having only one arm, would eliminate certain professions on a practical level, which narrowed my choices somewhat. Niël became a law student when he left school and I attended a few lectures with him. I wondered whether combining my interest in the medical field with law was a possibility.

In 1987 I completed Grade 12 with university exemption. The next year I enrolled as a law student at The University of Pretoria. Maybe one day, following in my grandfather's footsteps? Not always the most dedicated of students, the years ahead would be tough on me academically. In school I was more involved and interested in sports, and in a way, neglected the academic side. My mom was never sure when our exams started, or if I did indeed write exams. I did OK, taking into account that I hadn't spent too much time in front of my books. It was for that reason my parents were quite amazed when I got my results at the end of the year and my picture appeared on the front page of one of our local newspapers. As the case may be, the next year I would be a law student at one of the most well known universities in the country.

I was looking forward to being a law student. Maybe more for the social aspect and was a bit influenced by television programs like *LA Law*. I would however find out later that with more freedom came more responsibility.

I enjoyed my years as a law student, even though I sometimes struggled keeping up with the diversity and magnitude of subjects required to obtain my degree. Latin in itself kept me quite busy, to say the least. Following in Niël's footsteps also had its benefits, like always having the most reliable and complete notes at hand, consisting mostly of summaries from previous relevant court cases.

Although I struggled with a few subjects, I had my focus set on the day I would obtain my degree and become an attorney. With that goal I mind, I studied hard. Since I can remember, I have always been a fighter in all aspects of life, never willing to give up. With dedication and the constant prayers of my mom, I obtained my BLC degree in 1991, followed by my LLB degree in 1993.

The following year, I applied to several law firms to do my required articles as a candidate attorney. And although I had several interviews, I did not obtain the required position. At one of these interviews, one of the senior directors of a well known law firm wanted to know, for some or other reason, whether I was able to dress myself when going to work only having one arm. So much for equality, I thought. I soon found out that life out there is hard and tough. Everyone is only interested in fulfilling their own interests, and many are chasing their own dreams and fortunes.

Possessing a law degree, I was eventually appointed as a claims-handler at the Road Accident Fund (RAF) in 1993. In the three years I was employed at the RAF, dealing with claims instituted by attorneys on behalf of clients for injuries sustained in motor vehicle accidents, I gained a lot of experience with the civil litigation process as well as the diversity of injuries and its consequences. During my employment at the RAF, I attended law school in the evenings to adequately equip me for the legal world. With my focus set on becoming an attorney, I resigned from the RAF when I obtained a position as an article clerk at a law firm in the centre of Pretoria.

After completing my articles, I had to write the Attorneys Admission exams to become an admitted attorney. Passing this strenuous exam, I was admitted as an attorney of the High Court of South Africa in 1998, an achievement my grandfather, a former judge, was assuredly proud of. For the first year after being admitted, I was employed as a professional assistant mostly dealing with third party claims, acting for plaintiffs against the RAF.

Next, I accepted a position at a firm in Pretoria where I was employed for approximately one year.

In 2001, I resigned from the firm and opened my own practice. Since then, I have acted as the sole practitioner of my law firm doing mostly third party claims for injured victims.

As an attorney, I was confronted with the physical side of the occupation; climbing stairs, standing for hours in court and running around in the city on scorching summer days, serving and filing legal documents. Carrying heavy suitcases filled with files also put a strain on my prosthesis and the rest of my body. I never had the time to think about it though, sometimes working under tremendous pressure to do everything that's required to be done in a law firm. It was definitely nothing like *LA Law*. There was nothing glamorous about being an attorney, having to spend countless hours in stuffy, musky smelling court rooms and corridors. It's merely an occupation, like any other where one is bound to join the rat race to earn a decent living. An occupation and achievement however, that I am proud of.

On the other hand, it was a privilege to work with members of the public who had sustained injuries in accidents and went through the same emotional turmoil that I had experienced during my own ordeal. Knowing what they had gone through, and what they had experienced, made it easier relating to their pain and suffering and gave me a better understanding of their needs and uncertainties. Although I tried not to get emotionally involved with my clients, I could not help but sympathize with them, which in turn I believe, made me an even better attorney.

This career has become more of a calling than a job to me. Being successful on behalf of my clients and seeing smiles on their faces again, brings its own sense of satisfaction and achievement. Although not a job without occupational hazards, I love what I do and will keep on doing it for as long as possible. I am an attorney for the people.

18

GOING UNDER

WHILE A STUDENT, I was introduced to the world of scuba diving by a close friend. Fond of water sports, it didn't take a lot of persuasion to convince me that this was also something I would be interested taking on. Many years ago diving was an activity for the brave, the foolish and the downright stupid. The equipment used was unknown, so in fact these people were risking their lives to pave the way for us today, to safely enjoy this popular sport.

Initially, I was a bit unsure whether I would be able to cope with only one leg kicking against the currents, and whether it would affect my buoyancy underwater. I heard about paraplegics scuba diving and that gave me a boost of confidence.

My friend introduced me to members of the *Dolphin Diving School,* situated in the Garsfontein area in Pretoria East where he'd also done his course. They had all the facilities on site to conduct the theoretical part of the course as well as a heated swimming pool for the pool sessions. The diving instructor was confident that I would be able to complete the course according to NAUI rules and regulations. With that resounding endorsement I enrolled as one of their students in the Open Water Diver course and took the plunge.

Learning to dive has two phases. Phase one is knowledge development and pool training where you gain all the knowledge and skills necessary for safe diving. It starts with a lot of theory and a few lectures by the diving instructor from the textbook to prepare you for the written exam. Once the theoretical part is completed and you have passed the exam, you're eligible to join in the pool sessions, where you learn to become comfortable with the diving equipment. Once done with that, phase two is next where all the skills learned in phase one will be tested in the ocean training dives.

The theoretical part was quite tough but completely fascinating, learning how the gases affect your body and the effect the water pressure has on the oxygen in your lungs. We also learned how to use dive tables to calculate the level of carbon dioxide still present in the body after a dive. This was done to correctly plan for any further dive sessions and to avoid "the bends". We were warned about the always present, and lurking danger of Nitrogen narcosis, better known as "the narcs", resulting in under water hallucinations and sometimes even blackouts. The three golden rules of diving were drilled into our heads:

1. Equalize early and often;
2. Always exhale on emergency ascent;
3. Breathe continuously while scuba diving.

We learned about air and water pressure, density changes, buoyancy, vision, sound and air consumption. We also had to master the physiological part, learning about equalizing and the effect the water pressure has on the eardrums and the dangers of lung injuries; as well as the lurking danger of shallow water blackout and decompression sickness. We had to master assembling the equipment like tanks, regulators, *Octos* and *BCs* (buoyancy compensators).

During pool sessions, I soon discovered that scuba diving required optimum fitness levels. To qualify as an Open Water Diver, I was required to comply with the most stringent of tests, not only testing me physically, but mentally as well. I had to be able to swim a considerable amount of freestyle lengths in the pool, as well as underwater. Then we had to stay afloat without moving for a few minutes. Only after we had accomplished this, were we issued with diving equipment. In the five meter deep swimming pool we practiced all our skills to perfection. Buddy breathing, *DV* recovery and mask clearing underwater, became second nature after a few hours in the water. We'd each been issued with two regulators, the one for *DV* and the other, the *Octo* in case of an emergency if your buddy runs out of air.

I did my scuba diving course during the winter and we decided to rather do the qualifying dives in Bass Lake. The conditions there would be more favourable than at the East Coast at this time of the year.

With my mask, snorkels, fins, wetsuit, *DV*, *BC* , cylinders and determination, I arrived early one Saturday morning at Bass Lake with one purpose in mind, to pass the three required qualifying dives and register as a qualified scuba diver.

It was cold, and I quickly changed into my wetsuit for the first dive. I decided to leave my prosthetic leg on land, as it was a hassle underwater and affected my buoyancy. One leg should do the trick I thought. My friend helped me to the water and took the leg from me before I plunged into the water.

Bass Lake is an old dolomite mine which was closed down when it was flooded by fresh water. The water is clear and visibility fairly good. At the bottom of the lake, lies a thick layer of silt and when disturbed by scuba divers, makes the water murky. The spot is also used by police divers for training. At a maximum depth of about thirty meters, the lake is the perfect place for entry level divers to practice and get reacquainted with their skills. Obviously, and most importantly, a place to qualify.

Descending into the 11° dark water, I could feel the chill as the water entered my 5mm thick wetsuit, causing my heart to miss a beat or two. Although it was bitterly cold, I had to keep my mind on the skills I had learned. I had to show the instructor I had mastered the skills and I was ready to be qualified.

At a depth of about fifteen meters, I could see a grid under me while descending, equalizing frequently as I was taught when I felt the pressure of the water building on my eardrums. The students all sat in a circle on the grid, and we had to employ the skills we had been taught, over and over again. After roughly forty five minutes, we were given the hand signal from our instructor to start ascending slowly to the top. I survived and successfully completed my first dive.

The next day we completed the other two dives and in 1995 I qualified as an Open Water Diver, having completed all the requirements.

Almost like a driver's license, the real test only starts after qualifying.

The following year, my friend Phillip and I went down to Sodwana to gain further experience in scuba diving under unpredictable circumstances in the open ocean. He was already an advanced diver and had mastered most of the skills. There my theoretical knowledge about currents, surges and waves came in handy. Since then, I've completed more than forty five dives, most of them with my trusted dive buddy and friend. I have dived in all the favourite dive spots along the east coast of South Africa, like Protea Banks, T-Barge, Raggie Caves and Fontao Wreck, which are all situated close to Umhlanga.

As an amputee, the underwater world gave me an incredible sense of freedom, hanging weightlessly in the ocean surge. My friend however, humorously complained a few times of me losing direction, only kicking with one leg when we were diving in inland lakes.

Underneath the waves of the ocean, I found a world so peaceful and beautiful, only visible to those few who seek it out. A world filled with the most beautiful aspects life has to offer. Jacques Cousteau wrote: "No pen or tongue can describe the beauty of the underwater world." In this silent world, with only the constant sound of my own breathing through the regulator, I found a world unknown to many walking the surface of the earth. In this surreal and unusual world, I further found myself and my purpose for being on earth. Being one with God's creation, I felt so small and insignificant in those vast open spaces beneath the rolling waves of the majestic ocean. In a way, I was privileged to have experienced it. I had received a second chance in life, a chance not many have the privilege of getting. I knew that whatever came my way, I would be able to endure it if I placed my trust in God.

During my dives I have seen Moray eels, dolphins, sharks, water tortoises, stingrays, Potato bass and stonefish. The vibrant colours of the different kinds of angel fish were also breathtaking. Despite my ordeal a few years back, I felt so privileged to still be able to experience something that remains undiscovered by so many "average" people out there. I was whole in so many ways.

19

TRAVELLING ABROAD

IN THE YEAR 2001, I had the privilege of visiting the United States of America with my parents. At that time my sister Marilie and her husband were living abroad and we planned our trip carefully. We would fly directly to New York from South Africa, and our trip would take us to Seattle, then down the Californian coast and lastly to Atlanta.

During our trip I experienced the diversity of the world's third largest continent, North America, in its entire splendour with an unique blend of cultures and geographical variety. We had hotdogs from a street cart, saw the Statue of Liberty, visited the Empire State Building as well as Times Square in New York. We travelled from Seattle past Hollywood to romantic San Fransisco on the West Coast, through mountain ranges and past spectacular lakes and on to cosmopolitan cities. But most importantly, I experienced its people; fathers and mothers who had lost loved ones in one of the many battles fought; real people, with real feelings. Someone told me that there's probably not a single household in the USA that had not been affected by a family member who was either killed or maimed in battle. On 18 January 2007 there had already been at least 500 American amputees due to the Iraq War. The 500th victim was a twenty five year old man who lost both legs in a roadside bomb explosion. According to newspapers, the amputation rate for US troops in Iraq was twice that of past wars. In 2011 alone, they recorded 225 amputation cases in Afghanistan.

These people accepted me as one of their own without reservation. Wherever I went, doors at shopping malls were opened for me and my family and I never had to stand in a queue. They treated me as a war hero. It was so refreshing to experience their attitude towards life. An attitude of caring and giving, and expecting nothing in return. I learned a lot from the American people. I believe their attitude should be a lesson to us all...

LOSING AND FINDING LOVE

IKE ALL YOUNG boys, I showed very little interest in girls. That changed though when I started growing up. With hormone levels constantly changing, my interest started growing. When in Grade 5, my friends and I would invite girls to our birthday parties and soon after, Ring-around-the-Rosies turned into Spin-the-Bottle. In Grade 7, I was secretly and hopelessly in love with Paula, a girl from our athletics team, although she only found out about it months later. I used to send her messages through a mutual friend, to which she would reply in the same way. On Valentine's Day that year, I sent her flowers I had bought from a fellow pupil, and from that day on, at least for a while, we were boyfriend and girlfriend.

In high school I developed an even greater interest in the fairer sex. As an athlete, and being fairly popular amongst my friends, I soon built up healthy relationships with some of the girls at school. Many of them were only friends and we got along well. When the accident occurred I was still undergoing puberty, a time when a boy turns into a man. After the accident I had to adapt to and accept my changed body. Being healthy, young and strong at the time of the accident, played a critical role in my ability to regain muscle control and mobility. On the other hand, it made accepting my fate that much harder to endure, having always been a very physical person. I soon learned that, in order for someone else to accept and love me, I first had to accept and love myself. Out of the hospital, my self-esteem quickly returned when I found out that, although I had undergone some physical changes, I was still the same person and capable of doing anything I set my mind on. Life became a challenge. During our stay in the hospital, I received a lot of love and affection and many visits from Janine, my girlfriend at the time, with whom I had grown up. She had just returned with her family from Geneva where they had been living for a few years, when the accident occurred.

Out of hospital and back at school, I was treated like any other teenager and went through the same emotions and hardships that any teenager goes through. I had a few close relationships with girls and also had my heart broken a few times. I never saw myself as inferior to my peers, having lost limbs. The accident itself made me stronger and more confident in relationships. I realized that life was short and according to the odds, I should have died on that fateful day in 1984. Knowing this made me appreciate relationships even more than before. In Grade 10, I met and went out with Inger for a few months. She was always there when I started participating in sports for the disabled. She really boosted my confidence and was my best supporter!

After school I was single for a few months, but also had several female friends as fellow students. While at university, I would first focus my attention on studying and then on relationships. I met Karin with whom I went out for several months though.

In 1995, while employed at the RAF, I met my first wife. She was introduced to me by one of my colleagues. We were instantly attracted to each other. We dated for a few years, got engaged, and married in 1998. Unfortunately the marriage ended in divorce two and a half years later. The fact that a third party was involved was a severe blow to my self esteem.

Going through a divorce was probably one of the worst experiences of my life. I knew that I could deal with physical pain, having experienced it before, but this was something different. Being emotionally vulnerable at the time, the experience overwhelmed all my senses. I felt alone and lost. I spent hours trying to figure out what had gone wrong and where I had slipped up. I moved out of our house and stayed with a friend who lived close to work for a few weeks. During that time I focused all my attention on work, trying to clear my mind of the emotions that frequently threatened to overwhelm me. My life became dull, and I couldn't appreciate it anymore. I soon found myself a little apartment close to work that I rented from a lovely couple. There I spent many hours with my own thoughts over weekends, eating mostly take-away food and then again getting up early for work during the week and returning late.

Although these times were dark and lonely, it was definitely a necessary time to help me regain my self-confidence, and to face the fact that I would soon be divorced and on my own once more. I had the support of a loving family to help me through those times and a call from a family member on a lonely evening made all the difference. I knew that although I felt lonely and abandoned, I still had loved ones praying for, and thinking about me. My friend Phillip also paid me regular visits. He was there for me through both the good and the bad times.

During the divorce I struggled with my faith. I couldn't understand how God had allowed this to happen after the hardship of the accident I had to endure, and my ultimate acceptance. I would only later discover some of the reasons why.

I realized that I was vulnerable to bad experiences just like anyone else walking the face of the earth. When going through something we tend to focus all our attention on ourselves without seeing the bigger picture, but God never leaves us alone. We sometimes choose to climb out of His helping hand, trying to resolve our own problems.

Someone once said, "It is better to sail around Cape Point on a small sail boat during a storm with God, than on the Queen Mary, on a calm river without Him."

When the formal divorce proceedings were over, I felt alone but also relieved. Now it was time to take on the world again. The scars left by this endeavour I knew would eventually heal.

A few weeks after the divorce, I went out on a few "blind dates" arranged by my friends. During those times I met lovely and interesting people. But it was still difficult to regain trust in any relationship.

In 2001 a friend of mine, Marco, who was my prosthetist, invited me to move with him into a house in Constantia Park that he had purchased. Being back in the area I grew up in, and had lived for so many years, helped a lot in healing my emotional wounds. We shared the house with another guy. Everyone had his own tasks to keep the household and the commune going. It was in 2001 that I started my own legal practice from home, working in an encouraging and uplifting environment. And whenever I needed work done to my prosthesis, Marco was close by, also practicing from home, to do the necessary.

In 2002 I was invited to a dinner at the house of a mutual friend. One of the guys staying in our house took along his girlfriend, a former model, whom he had met a few weeks before. They also invited her friend Ronel, whom I'd heard about, but never met before.

Everyone arrived with their companions at the dinner party. Ronel arrived a bit later in my friend's car. When I saw her, I was immediately attracted to this energetic person with the lively greenish eyes. She was a bit reserved initially but I soon broke through the barrier and had an open conversation with her. We talked as if we had been friends for years. Sitting on the balcony outside, she told me about her involvement in the modelling business, and I shared my life's story with her. I was intrigued by her interest in all aspects of life, and could not help but focus all my attention on her. As a quick judge of character, I soon realized that she had all the characteristics I wanted in a woman. She was beautiful inside out. Trying not to show too much affection, I sat next to her at the dinner table, as she had offered to serve me my food. The evening went by in a flash and everyone left, all going their separate ways. I told Ronel that I would probably see her again with her being a friend of my friend's girlfriend. In my heart I knew I would see her again!

Ronel accepted a position at a hair salon and I got hold of her cell phone number. A few weeks later, on the evening before she started work at the new place, I gave her a call wishing her the best of luck. In her voice I could hear amazement, probably because I remembered when she would start at her new job.

A few days later I arranged a movie night at our place and invited Ronel to join in. Again I could feel the attraction when I saw her. We spent the evening laughing and chatting. My attention wasn't on the movie. I can't even remember the title of the movie we watched. When it was time for her to leave, I suddenly felt the urge to kiss her. She saw it coming and turned her cheek. I realized that to win her heart I would have to be the best hunter out there.

Being the hunter I am, I invited her to have coffee with me and she accepted my invitation. As we sat inside Burgundy's, a cosy coffee shop, we had a lengthy conversation about every aspect of life. I could not take my eyes off hers. I knew in my heart that I had found my soul mate. That evening when I took her home, she welcomed my kiss and I was more in love than ever before.

Our relationship grew by the minute, and driving to and from my house to her apartment in the city soon became part of my routine.

In 2004 we went down to visit my parents in Ballito on the Kwazulu Natal North coast for the weekend. I however, had alternative plans in mind. I planned the evening down to the smallest detail. After walking on the beach for a while, Ronel and I sat down on the rocks overlooking the incoming waves. I had her ring tucked away in my pocket and we had a picnic basket with us. I told her that we were going to have a sundowner on the beach. We sat in silence for a while, my heart pounding in my chest, repeating in my mind the best way to say it. Without further ado, I broke the silence. I asked her in a trembling voice if she would be my future wife and the future Mrs Louw. She looked up at me with tears of joy in her beautiful eyes and accepted my proposal without hesitation. By that time we were both teary eyed as I embraced her. We were the luckiest couple on this earth.

My parents, who were in on the surprise, then arrived as planned. We shared a bottle of sparkling wine in celebration while the orange glow of the sun slowly disappeared over the breaking waves. The night set in, and the moon lit the phosphor in the foam forming around the rocks. Another day had gone by and we had so much to be grateful for.

On 3 September 2005, a day I will never forget, Ronel and I had the most wonderful wedding in Ballito at The Waterberry, a popular local coffee shop and wedding venue. We only invited our closest family and friends and the event was small and intimate. Our dream of having a wedding in Kwazulu Natal on the North coast became true on that hot spring morning under an open blue sky. This was the day I married my princess. As she walked down the aisle in her beautiful wedding dress, I could barely keep my emotions under control. God had given me so much more than I expected and asked for. Ronel and I said our wedding vows in the presence of our loved ones, surrounded by the most beautiful setting of green indigenous trees and the peaceful rumblings of the waves in the distance. What an emotional experience it was! I love her deeply.

We moved into a comfortable duet in Faerie Glen, Pretoria, close to the area where I grew up and had stayed with Marco for a while. It was a place where we could relax and unload after a strenuous day at work. I had found my soul mate and best friend. Since we met, we've learned to work as a team in whatever we do. Ronel is my companion and right hand, strong in her beliefs, and confident in her approach to life. She loves life, but even more importantly, she loves God and she loves me.

FAMILY VALUES

SINCE MY MARRIAGE to Ronel we have had a lot of fun, success and laughter together. Unfortunately we've had to endure the passing of her mother and grandfather recently. Sometimes I wish I could take her pain on myself and spare her. But the bad in life also tends to draw people closer. Other obstacles have also passed our way and we have had to deal with them, just like we will deal with any more that comes our way. That's all part of life. We grow daily as people, partners and co-travellers in this world. It's however, such a great privilege to share life with the one I love. My wife has never seen me as a disabled person. In her eyes, I am whole and her husband. She will sometimes ask me to hold onto more than one thing, forgetting that I only have one hand. We work and play and plan tasks together.

When obstacles come our way and rocks are rolled onto our path, and our house is shaken, Ronel is the one that keeps everything calm and collected. I have learned a lot from her in the years gone by.

Ronel is the one that will come home with a dove with a broken wing in her hands. And against all odds, she will try and save it. She's the one that goes out of her comfort zone and sees the needs of others, especially the elderly who cross her path. Since I've met Ronel, I've seen her grow into a strong-willed and determined woman despite difficult obstacles she'd endured as a little girl. We must learn from the mistakes of others, we must learn to forgive and forget, even though it is sometimes painful. She taught me to forgive and forget, in order to experience total freedom.

In 2007 Ronel and I visited the Spice Island of Zanzibar, a semi-autonomous part of Tanzania, East Africa. This popular tropical holiday destination's main industries consist of spices – cloves , pepper and cinnamon – raffia and tourism. The whole island is 32 km wide and 108 km in length. It is characterized by white sandy beaches beneath beautiful indigenous palm trees, coral reefs and old historical sites. Those coral reefs are well known by scuba divers and snorkelers alike.

The island is mostly populated by African people like the Swahili. They are well known for their friendliness and hospitality despite their poor lifestyle in small villages. They mostly fish and farm to earn a living. The Swahili are also very artistic and tourists can buy their local paintings around every corner and on all beaches. What I loved about the island was not only the friendliness of the inhabitants, but also their will to survive despite adversities. We have talked to many of the locals and were overwhelmed by their positive outlook in life. In Stone Town, a small Swahili girl was not afraid or intimidated by my prosthesis, and I took photographs of her clinging onto my leg, much to the amusement of onlookers. She had probably never seen an artificial limb before. It is a truly wonderful place, with wonderful people that makes for a very romantic vacation.

In 2010 we visited Namibia as a family. Ronel and I went with my Jeep Wrangler Sahara. This was the first real test for my yuppie 4x4 I bought in 2008, as I had been city bound until then. We drove on tough gravel roads and my dad told us that driving those roads separated the boys from the men. One afternoon we were driving in convoy against the setting sun. My brother Niël and his wife Hannelie in front, followed by my dad and mom in their SUV, and Ronel and I in third place, followed by my sister Marilie and her husband Jaco in their vehicle. I totally misjudged one of the *cattle grids* as a result of the poor visibility caused by the setting sun and the dust, and was suddenly faced with a fence about ten meters away at a speed of approximately 90km/h. All I could do was slam on the brakes and turn the steering wheel as hard as I could to try and bring the vehicle to a halt. We stopped uninjured about 30cm parallel to the fence. This again made us realize how quickly things can go wrong and how short life can be. We were saved once more. I also developed some serious respect for my Jeep Wrangler. We must learn to spend time with God in our everyday activities, because He is constantly present. We need to learn to seek God's face in our surroundings. In the vast open spaces of a desert and in the intimacy of indigenous forests, God is indeed visible. I always feel closer to God in nature, where I can experience His constant presence in His beautiful creation.

In 2012, I again had the opportunity to visit the USA, this time with my wife Ronel. We stayed with friends in Connecticut on the East Coast. Once again I experienced the warmth of the people and their caring attitude. We visited New York by train a couple of times and conquered the subways. On Christmas Eve, a few local residents came by, singing Christmas carols, standing out there in the snow in front of the house we stayed in. I was privileged enough to join a small prayer group with my friend on the day before we left. It was eye opening to experience the genuine depth of faith these people had despite catastrophes like 9/11 and the Sandy Hook massacre. I was welcomed into their group with open arms as a fellow Christian and brother in Christ. We spent a few hours in prayer and devotion that morning, next to a frozen river with a *Starbucks* sign in the background. It's a moment I will cherish for the rest of my life.

During my visit to *Ratanga Junction*, an amusement park in Cape Town a few years ago, I wanted to buy tickets for one of the rides. The queue was about 100 meters long. I asked my brother to go and find out if I had to stand in the queue or if they would accommodate someone with an artificial leg. He returned twenty minutes later with the news that I could go on the ride, but that I had to stand in the queue. I didn't expect preferential treatment, just fairness. Unfortunately, fairness does not exist in many aspects of society in our country.

My wife and I decided to take on the Cape Cobra at *Ratanga Junction* without consent. This well known rollercoaster ride offers an exhilarating experience of speeds close to 100 km/h and 360⁰ degree turns. When we got into the front cart we had to remove all our loose items. Needless to say, I had to take off my artificial limb as well. The ride was everything it promised to be. I can still remember the astonished faces of the next group of people waiting in line when they saw me approaching without my prosthetic leg.

During the recent elections in our country, I was told by an official that I could skip the rest of the line for the voting booth after having already stood in the queue for over an hour. My wife however, would not be allowed to skip the line with me. I could not see the purpose then. As I have previously said, I do not expect to be treated differently, just with fairness.

A few years ago I started riding motorcycles again, despite the pact my mom and I had made years ago that I would get rid of motorcycles as soon as I got my driver's license for my car. This time I had to get my wife's permission. Ronel gave me the green light and I got myself a 125cc on/off road motocross bike. Being the adrenalin junkie that I am, I needed the bike as a way to get rid of normal daily stress. I did the conversion myself and quickly got the hang of it again after so many years of not riding. The problem however, started when I got too relaxed with my riding ability. I lost concentration and then control of the bike. I stumbled head first over the handle bars onto the tar and fell right in front of an astonished onlooker walking by. He went on minding his own business as I got up after finding my prosthesis lying next to me. I inspected my wounds and realized I hadn't broken anything. I phoned Ronel to tell her of my accident but before I could mention it, she told me that she was busy with a client. That evening at home she wanted to know why I was limping and I told her about the fall. Since then, whenever I call, the first thing she asks is whether I am OK before telling me that she's busy.

The wonderful thing is that my wife understands me and I understand her.

When I recently purchased a new motor vehicle, the sales person insisted on a test drive and went with me. On our way to the highway, I told him that whenever I got into a new car, I first had to get used to the distance between the brake and the petrol, because I was driving with a prosthesis. To get some reaction from him, I told him that I sometimes get a little confused between the pedals because I could not feel them. We had a very short test drive...

GLANCING BACK

LOOKING BACK OVER the years, I can only bow down before my Creator in deep gratitude for how my life turned out to be. I believe that each one of us is born with certain strengths and characteristics. I would never have been able to cope with everything that was thrown on my path with only my own strength. I had to give the controls over to God. Clearly, when there was only one set of footprints, God was carrying me .

I also became intensely aware of the value of the assistance and love from family members and friends. They formed an integral part of the recuperation and rehabilitation process, and ultimately in achieving success. When I had to physically cope with the pain and suffering, my family coped with the emotional pain of going through it with me, ultimately resulting in even stronger family bonds. On this earth, each one of us is placed, not in a position of isolation, but in a network of interactions between different role players in our lives, each one with his or her own task of building or sometimes, unfortunately, breaking down and destroying our inner selves. As the saying goes, "You cannot choose your family but you can at least choose your friends..." I was fortunate to have been born into a family where I learned the value of love and affection at a very early age. Not everyone is that fortunate, but you still have the choice of choosing who you want to spend time with. God gave us the wonderful, but sometimes difficult ability to make choices. We should trust Him in all our choices because, when we feel abandoned and alone, God is still with us.

I am still an athlete, competing in the race of life. The experiences I've had, both good and bad, definitely played a part in shaping me into the person I am today. As an athlete, I am certainly aware of the intense amount of exercise and practice one has to apply in order to win the race. And although winning isn't everything, I will always keep on trying.

Thinking back on the accident, everyone put on my path had his or her role to play. The paramedics, the doctors, the nurses and all the other hospital personnel, to name a few. Each did their best to save my life, and to help me adapt to my new body. I am what I am today, as a result of the dedication and enthusiasm of many people, each with their own area of expertise.

It is only when we realize that each of us walking the face of the earth has a purpose for being here, that we find comfort and acceptance in everything that comes our way, the whole time keeping in mind that there is a bigger picture. Only then can we use every opportunity to our advantage, enhancing each experience. We have to keep on looking at the bigger picture and not the storm in the tea cup.

Going through this experience, I have learned a lot about myself. I have gained a language I can use to encourage others going through the same kinds of experiences. Whenever I see another amputee, I feel a kind of brotherly love towards them, knowing that we share the same language. Niël and I have also visited many other amputees who were still in the hospital, to give them a few words of encouragement. I can still remember the people who visited us in hospital, who went through similar operations, and the way in which their words encouraged us. They already knew the language we were just starting to learn...

Something I had to get used to was the inquisitive and curious stares of members of the public, especially when walking on a beach in my swimming trunks. So many people have approached me, telling me how brave I am for taking on life, despite of my disability. Some people will openly ask questions while others will only stare in awe and disbelief. I gained a lot of experience in life by the way other people react towards something out of the ordinary. In the past, I always blended in with the crowd.

Being a witness of God's love out there in the world in itself makes me feel privileged – sometimes without even having to say a word. Children will approach me, touching my artificial limb, asking outright questions, most often to the embarrassment of their parents. I have learned to accept and appreciate the attention I receive in these situations, making the best of every opportunity and answering all the curious questions people may have. In a way, as a result of the ever expanding media cover of athletes' participation in sport for the disabled, artificial limbs and people with amputations have become more common and every day in our modern society.

As a student, my friends and I toured Zimbabwe for two weeks. We visited the tourist attractions like Victoria Falls where we signed up for a river rafting expedition down the Zambezi River. The mighty Zambezi River was in full flow that year. Although initially a bit uncertain as to whether I would be able to join my friends in this activity, having heard about all the precautions one had to take and release forms that had to be signed, as well as the fear of losing my prosthesis in the rumbling waters, I decided to go when encouraged by my friends. It turned out to be a very physical activity, and we had to hold on to the rope around the rubber duck and dive from one side of the boat to the other to keep it from capsizing. My friends got a few cuts and bruises from my prosthesis but had no complaints. What a spectacular experience it was.

Every day brings new opportunities and challenges and I've learned to take them on with all my might, and to put my trust in God.

Obviously, I also have my down days, otherwise called *bad hair days*, when I wish things had been a bit different. Like getting out of bed without first having remembered to put on my leg, or not having to worry about the constant danger of getting pressure sores when walking long distances. I realize how many times in life we take what we have for granted.

On the other hand, being optimistic made things a lot easier to endure. Personality and positive thinking also play a huge roll. The whole idea of having to go through life on a prosthetic limb, only became another challenge for me. For someone else it may have become a huge burden. It all depends on your outlook on life. Going to the gym and doing leg presses with 120 kilogram weights, tested both my endurance and strength, as well as the strength and quality of my prosthetic limb. Many times I left the gym with a broken artificial foot or screw. Luckily I always had spare parts handy, and sometimes fixed the leg myself, not always having a prosthetist nearby. I am quite amazed by the way in which the modern prosthesis can allow one to live a normal life with only a small amount of alteration here and there.

And then of course there are the famous amputees like Rick Allen, the drummer for the British rock band Def Leppard, who stayed in the band after losing his left arm in an accident. Bethany Hamilton, the American surfer who lost her arm in a shark attack and still kept on surfing; Aimee Mullins, an American athlete and model, who despite having had both legs amputated, kept her dream going and became a world record holder in athletics. Terry Fox, a Canadian athlete, who despite the fact that his right leg was amputated above the knee, ran across Canada to raise money for cancer research and is considered one of Canada's greatest heroes.

Hennie, Niël and I decided a few years ago to start a club for amputees. The idea was that amputees would come together and share their experiences and difficulties, as well as their triumphs in life in an environment of understanding of fellow amputees. We placed the following ad in the local newspaper:

"AMPUTATION CLUB – If you've lost a limb and would consider joining a club, call …"

We only received one response to our ad. Someone called and told us that he was a rock and semi-precious stone collector. He wanted to know what kind of stone an "Amputation" was. Needless to say, we decided against the idea. I think many people are uncomfortable with being categorized into a certain group and understandably so. Sometimes all of us just want to blend in.

Stories of great achievements by disabled people like summiting Kilimanjaro in a wheel chair, and completing the Comrades Marathon on two artificial limbs warms the heart and inspires the soul. It motivates even me to greater achievements in all aspects of life. We are what we are as a result of our achievements, and the difficulties we have learned to overcome. Life would have been boring without a challenge now and then. Many of the well known heroes of today who left legacies behind to follow, were confronted by some kind of difficulty in their lives which they had to endure and overcome.

You cannot separate life from what you believe in. In other words, everything that happens to us on this earth, is in a way, directly linked to our beliefs and eternity. When writing a book about your life, it is impossible to do so without reference to what you believe in. Life without belief does not make sense.

Writing this book made me realize how fortunate I am, being able to live life in abundance. I had to dig deep into the emotional turmoil of years gone by and in a way relived some of those experiences as I put it into words. I have received a second chance in life. What I do with it is up to me alone. God granted me the ability of choice. I have chosen to follow Him and to make the best of every opportunity, to broaden my experience on this planet, and to never ever give up. What you decide is up to you.

AFTERTHOUGHT

OVER THE LAST 30 years since the accident in 1984 I have experienced so many blessings in my life and I have met many wonderful people to share them with, some of whom I would never have met was it not for the accident. Our normal daily tasks can become extraordinary when we look for the meaning behind normal every day activities in our lives and the reason for our existence. Everyone has a purpose to fulfil. God does not make mistakes. I feel so privileged being in this situation and for the path that was chosen for me. My journey through life without an arm and a leg is relatively short, if you take into account the wider picture of eternity.

I trust and believe that God has used my story to the benefit of others. I pray that my life and my trust in God will continue to inspire and motivate people in such a way, that they will be able to motivate those around them to greater victory. We were meant to leave a legacy behind.

How will people remember you?

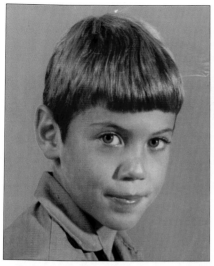

In Grade Four at Skuilkrans Primary School.

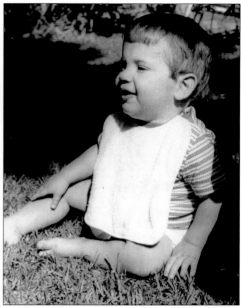

Happy baby.

Niël, Marilie and I.

At the crèche developing my artistic side.

This photo was taken by my brother Niël approximately 5 minutes before the accident - with me sitting front left, Cronnie sitting in front with the cap and Hennie standing at the back.

Rand Daily Mail 29/12/84

Grim blow for 3 brave boys

BRAAM LOUW
Lost an arm and a leg

Mail Reporter

PRETORIA'S three "catamaran boys" lay in their hospital beds yesterday, gamely discussing how they would overcome their handicaps.

Two of the boys lost an arm, while a third lost an arm and a leg after the aluminium mast of the catamaran they were launching at the Swartvlei Lake in the George-Knysna area in the Cape touched an 11 000-volt cable.

The limbs were amputated at the H F Verwoerd Hospital.

Holiday horror

Neil Louw, 16, and his brother Braam, 15, of Freeborn Road, the Willows, and their friend Hennie Beukes of Saligna Street, Lynnwood Ridge, are recuperating in Ward 12, where they received frequent visits from family and friends yesterday.

"We are impressed by their strength", said Mrs Ansie Beukes after seeing them.

"They are telling each other how they are going to work on overcoming their handicaps. They won't let the amputations get them down."

The boys each lost an arm, while Braam, who was severely injured, also lost a leg.

All three were good rugby players and athletes at Die Wilgers Hoërskool.

The two families live about a block apart and have known each other for years. Mr Gert Beukes, a personnel manager, and Mrs Petro Louw, who works at a creche, went to school together. She is married to Mr Jacques Louw, a scientist.

Cronie Beukes, 15, who was on the craft during the accident but who escaped unhurt, was also at the hospital to visit his brother Hennie. But he seemed close to tears and could not describe the accident.

Mrs Louw said there were no notices to warn people of the overhead powerlines at the lake.

NEIL LOUW
Lost an arm

Seuns net dankbaar dat hul nog lewe

Mei 1985

DANIE KLOPPER

PRETORIA — Die verlore seuns van Die Wilgers is weer terug in hul ou gewaad — uitgevat in skoolklere en getrou op hul pos om die akademie soos van ouds weer vierkantig in die oë te staar.

En kan die twee standerd neges, Neil Louw, 17, Hennie Beukes, 16, en Neil se jonger broer Braam Louw, 15, wat in standerd agt is, nie vir 'n vale praat en beduie nie.

Hul dankbaarheid dat hulle nog lewe en die manier waarop hulle mekaar om die beurt in die rede val om jou te vertel van hul onvergeetlike ondervinding in Desember verlede jaar, toe hulle van hul ledemate moes inboer, laat jou skoon verbysterd in jou voetspore vassteek.

Met ongeloof luister jy na die drie seuns se verhaal, wat teruggaan na Welwillendheidsdag, toe elk van hulle 'n elektriese skok van 11 000 volt opgedoen het ná hul tweeromp-seiljag se mas met 'n hoogspanningsdraad in aanraking gekom het.

Die ongeluk waarin die seuns op 'n nippertjie na noodlottig beseer is, het op die Swartvleimeer tussen Wildernis en Knysna in Suid-Kaapland plaasgevind.

Die elektriese stroom het die seuns

Die drie seuns van Die Wilgers, Braam Louw, 15, sy vriend Hennie Beukes, 16 en ouer bro[er Neil Louw,] 17, by die tweeromp-seiljag (Hal Cat) waarop hulle op Welwillendheidsdag verlede jaa[r] nippertjie na noodlottig beseer is.

Af arms en af been keer [n]ie glimlagge

Deur DAWIE VAN HEERDEN: Pretoria

NEIL en Hennie het elk 'n regterarm verloor. Braam sy regterbeen en regterarm. Maar waar die drie skoolseuns van Pretoria in die hospitaal lê, sien jy [n]et glimlagge. Die drie is vol grappe. En vol moed.

Dit is hierdie moed, en hul deursettingsvermoë en opgeruimdheid, wat die ouers van sestienjarige Neil Louw en sy broer, Braam, 15, en van hul boesemvriend, Hennie Beukes, 16, nuwe krag gee vir die moeilike pad wat nou voorlê.

...seuns glo dit is 'n ...t met hulle moet ge...et. Hulle weet dit is ... nuwe lewe wat vir ...voorlê, maar hulle ... vorentoe. Hulle is ... en sterk. Dit is in ...al 'n wonderwerk ...e nog leef," sê mnr. ... Louw, Neil en ...e pa.

Drade

...y en my vrou, Pe... Hennie se ouers ...n geweldige slag ... egter baie beter ... die seuns in die ...besoek het. Hulle ...uwe moed gegee ...ositiewe benade... hulle aan die dag ... Louw.

...ie seuns is ... ernstig beseer ...ektriese stroom ... volt deur hulle ... Hulle was besig ...eromp-seiljag na ...vleimeer naby ...e stoot toe die ...aan hoogspan...aak.

...is na die hospitaal op George gebring voordat hulle per ambulansvliegtuig na die H.F. Verwoerd-Hospitaal in Pretoria oorgeplaas is. Hulle het in die hospitaal op George al geweet dat van hul ledemate afgesit gaan word.

Nie bewus

En in die vliegtuig op pad na Pretoria het hulle vir mekaar gebid.

NEIL LOUW

BRAAM LOUW

Intussen is daar op Sedgefield bewerings dat die seuns hul seiljag onwettig te water probeer laat het. Die stadsklerk, mnr. Reg Basson, sê sover hy weet behoort die grond rondom die Swartvleimeer, waar die ongeluk gebeur het, aan private eienaars wat toegangsgeld vra vir betreding.

"Die seuns het die jag te water gelaat op 'n plek waar niemand dit eintlik behoort te doen nie," sê hy.

Mnr. Louw sê as die seuns oortree het, was hulle nie eens daarvan bewus nie. Hy glo ook nie hulle het verkeerd gedoen nie, want 'n oop hek het toegang verleen tot die plek waar hulle wou gaan seil.

● Die NG gemeente van Lynnwoodrif, Pretoria, het besluit om 'n hulpfonds vir die seuns te stig. Die opbrengs sal die hoë mediese koste help dek. Bydraes kan gestuur word aan Die NG Kerkkantoor Lynnwoodrif, Posbus 20130, Alkantrant, 0005.

Volksblad 28/2/84

Drie verloor elk arm in ongeluk

Eie Beriggewer

PRETORIA. — Drie skoolseuns van Pretoria het elk 'n arm en een 'n been verloor deurdat hulle 'n elektriese skok van 11 000 volt opgedoen het toe die mas van hul tweeromp-seiljag aan 'n hoogspanningsdraad vasgehaak het.

Die kortsluiting wat daardeur naby Sedgefield in Oos-Kaapland veroorsaak is, het die dorp sowat 'n uur sonder krag gelaat.

Die regterarm en regterbeen van Braam Louw (15) van Freebornstraat 326 in die spogvoorstad Die Wilgers in Pretoria is afgesit. In 'n poging om sy broer, Neil (16), en hul vriend, Hennie Beukes van Selingnastraat 310,

NEIL LOUW

Lynnwoodrif, te help, is Braam die ernstigste beseer. Neil en Hennie het elk 'n regterarm verloor.

Die ledemate is gister oggend in die H. F. Verwoerd-hospitaal in Pretoria afgesit nadat die drie seuns eergisternag met 'n ambulansvliegtuig van die Rooi Kruis in Kaapstad van die hospitaal op George na Pretoria gebring is.

Die grusame fratsongeluk het Woensdagmiddag omstreeks twee-uur gebeur. Die seuns wou op die Swartvleimeer tussen Knysna en Wildernis gaan vaar. Hennie Beukes se boer, Kronie (17), was ook by.

Die parkeergebied by die brug oor die meer, waar skuite normaalweg gereed gemaak word, was vol. Die seuns het besluit om hul jag oorkant die nasionale pad vir die vaart voor te berei en dit op 'n sleepwa na die water te stoot. Die boot se mas is onder meer opgesit.

Terwyl Braam en Kronie op die mat tussen die rompe van die seiljag gesit het, het Neil en Hennie die boot na die ander kant van die pad gesleep, het Braam ná die ongeluk aan hospitaalpersoneel op George vertel. Hulle was skynbaar onbewus van die kragdrade langs die pad en die aluminium-maspaal het aan die drade geraak.

BRAAM LOUW

Die mas is met staalkabels aan 'n aluminiumrand om die boot vas. Die kragtige stroom het Neil en Hennie van pyn laat gil toe dit hulle tref.

Braam en Kronie het verskrik van die jag afgespring. Braam het geprobeer om Neil en Hennie te help, maar voordat die veiligheidskakelaar die krag afgeskakel het, het hy ernstiger brandwonde as die ander twee opgedoen.

Vervolg op bl. 2

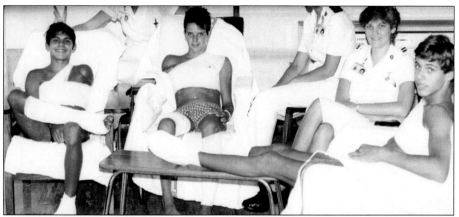

The three of us in hospital after our transferral from the intensive care unit.

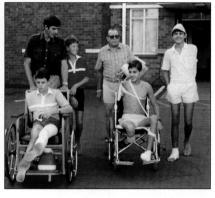

Moedige seuns
gaan huis toe!

Above: Leaving hospital.

Elk kort 'n arm, ryk aan talente

CARLIEN GROBBELAAR

HULLE boer op die tennisbane, is elke dag in die gimnasium en ryg medaljes vir atletiek in. Waar kattekwaad aangevang word, is hulle by — die enigste verskil is net dat Hennie Braam (16) Louw

... dermate verloor ná ... idsdag in 1984 toe ... op die Swartvlei- ... er wou laat en die ... de geraak het. Die ... van sowat 11 000

... e Suid-Afrikaanse ... ir gestremdes in ... n Braam het hier ... se rekord in atle- ... des verbeter. ... ransvaal-kleure in ... y die Atletiekver- ... erwerf

... stasies in die 100m ... spiesgooi, gewig- ... tremdes verwerf ... ir die Staatspresi- ... ade-dekorasie van ... het Neil en Hen- ... eluk te hulp gesnel ... l-kleure vir skyf- ... ooi gekry ... 1 500m en 800m

... eenkomste vir ge- ... moedige seuns die

... skool aan gewone ... ier laat hulle die ... s onlangs aan die ... ns in Pretoria vir ... geneem.

HIERDIE drie seuns laat atletiekrekords by die dosyne tuimel, al het elkeen net een arm. Hennie Beukes (links) en Braam en Neil Louw neem nou aan die Suid-Afrikaanse junior sportbyeenkoms vir gestremdes in Bloemfontein deel en Neil en Braam het al elk 'n Suid-Afrikaanse rekord vir gestremdes verbeter.

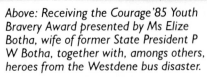

Above: Receiving the Courage '85 Youth Bravery Award presented by Ms Elize Botha, wife of former State President P W Botha, together with, amongs others, heroes from the Westdene bus disaster.

My sister Marilie holding the Woltemade Decoration for Bravery, and also several gold medals awarded to me at an athletic event for the disabled.

Niël (left) Hennie (middle) Braam (right).

Hennie, with myself and my parents. In front: my sister Marilie and brother Niël.

On my Kawazaki in 2015.

My parents Jacques and Petro in Ballito.

My lovely wife, Ronel, on our wedding day in Ballito.